THE ROAR OF MY SILENCE

ANKIT BAGDI

Made with ♥ on the Notion Press Platform
www.notionpress.com

To all **women**

who are beautiful in their rights.

You are an Inspiration.

Each one of You.

May your stories be heard,

your dreams be realized,

and your voices be celebrated.

Contents

Foreword   *vii*

Acknowledgements   *ix*

Preface   *xi*

Prologue   *xiii*

1. Enduring Shadows: The Judge, The Audience, And The Reluctant Bride   1

2. Lotus In A Co-Ed Garden   8

3. Raindrops And Culinary Delights: Unveiling Mandav's Treasures   12

4. Shadows Of Solitude: Desires Unveiled   21

5. The Distant Drumbeats Of Destiny   23

6. The Weight Of Expectations: The Complexities Of A New Life   36

7. Love's Delicate Flame   41

8. Boundaries Of Strength   46

9. Unspoken Tensions And The Road Ahead"   51

10. Bound By Love, Guided By Resilience   54

11. Echoes Of Destiny"   59

12. Destiny: The Radiant Red And The Airtel Register   62

13. Tangled Emotions   67

14. The Veil: Tainted Vegetables And Confined Desires"   69

15. Crossroads Of Confessions   72

16. A Doll's Imprisonment: Marital Rape And Desperate Yearnings   78

Contents

17. Love - Whispers In The Enchanted Garden   81

18. Finding Hope In Unexpected Places   87

19. Veiled Flames: Love's Unraveling Thread   91

20. The Gaze That Beckoned   96

21. Embracing Motherhood,Embracing Strength   98

22. Serendipitous Encounters On The Midnight Train   104

23. A Battle Of Hearts: Confronting Love And Tradition   107

24. Ink Of Love: Crafting Our Union On Paper   112

25. When Time Stood Still: A Mother's Battle For Life   116

26. Embracing Motherhood's Beautiful Chaos   122

27. Echoes Of Silence   126

28. Silent Whispers: Seeking The Name Of Fate   129

29. Love Beyond Dowry   131

30. Whispers Of Fate   133

31. The Weight Of Silence   136

32. Shadows Of Desperation   139

33. Embracing The Sunrise Of Freedom   142

34. Destiny's Embrace   148

35. Bound By An Invisible Thread   151

36. Courage Amid Chaos: A Battle For Freedom And Happiness   160

37. Defying Judgment, Embracing Freedom: A Divorcee's Journey   165

38. Raindrops Of Intimacy:Unveiling Mandav's Secrets   169

Foreword

Whenever you read a good book, somewhere in the world, a door opens to spread light. This book will definitely open the light of a new thought for women in the minds of men.

--Amitabh Bachchan

The anecdote of the book would not let you breathe. It's a well-braided story that reinforces the reader to flip through pages. The kind of a woman's life depicted in the novel provides the reader with a touching view of what life can be for women. The sentiments of this book are tear-demanding ones.

- NIGHAT ABBASS
Social Worker ,Delhi

Acknowledgements

First and foremost, I would like to express my deepest gratitude to Lord Shiv. Throughout the process of putting this book together, I have come to realize how truly blessed I am to have the gift of writing. Through Mahakal's divine guidance and unwavering support, I can believe in my passion and pursue my dreams. This book would not have come to fruition without my faith in Shiv. Thank you for everything.

I am also indebted to the countless individuals who have directly and indirectly supported and influenced me on this journey. Your contributions have been invaluable, and I would like to take a moment to acknowledge each of you.

To my family, thank you for always standing by my side and providing me with the love and encouragement I needed. Your unwavering belief in me has been the driving force behind my success.

To my friend Raunak, thank you for being there for me through the ups and downs, lending an ear when I needed to vent, and reminding me of the importance of perseverance. Your friendship has been a constant source of strength.

I am humbled and honoured to have had the opportunity to bring this book to life. To everyone who has played a part, big or small, in making this dream a reality, thank you from the bottom of my heart. Your belief in me and your unwavering support has been the foundation for this book.

Preface

Women, the remarkable and intricate members of the human species, are indispensable in perpetuating love and life on our planet.

"The Roar of My Silence" unveils the tale of a girl named Kumudh, affectionately known as "Superwomen" by yours. Her struggle is ceaseless as she valiantly contends to inhale the invigorating air of freedom.

Let me clarify something about Kumudh: she is not your typical superwoman who soars through the skies or engages in epic battles like a comic book heroine. Instead, Kumudh is an ordinary girl who transforms into a genuine "superwoman".

Through Kumudh's journey, I aim to provide a transparent and authentic portrayal of a society that many of us—living in bustling urban centres and viewing India as a rapidly progressing nation—might find difficult to understand.

The question lingers: Is she on a trajectory toward a future better than the one she is leaving behind?

(Immerse yourself in the narrative, and reciting the significant "dates" will heighten your reading experience.)

Prologue

The faint, delicate purple scar etched across my abdomen serves as a lasting symbol of how my precious son, "AARAV," entered this world through a necessary cesarean section. It's reminiscent of a second birth canal, a remarkable six inches in length—yes, I admit, I measured it! It never ceases to astound me how a tiny opening could accommodate the passage of a beautiful life. But in the grand scheme of things, I've realised that his arrival method is inconsequential. What truly matters is that he exists before me, thriving and full of life. When I gaze upon "AARAV," the manner of his birth fades into insignificance, eclipsed by the sheer joy of his presence in my life.

August 2013 (Evening at 10 PM)

My stomach growled loudly, a reminder that I was pregnant and desperately needed to eat. With a deep sigh, I went to the kitchen, hoping to find something to satisfy my hunger. To my dismay, there was nothing readily available. The cabinets were bare, and the pantry offered no solace. My gaze landed on the refrigerator, a glimmer of hope in an otherwise empty kitchen.

Fear crept over me like a shadow as I approached the fridge. My mother-in-law's strict rules echoed in my mind, reminding me that I could not touch anything in this house. I couldn't even adjust the air conditioner or use the remote control, let alone open the fridge. But with hunger gnawing at my insides, I couldn't ignore the desperate craving any longer.

Trepidation filled my trembling hands as I reached for the fridge handle. I hesitated, unsure of what awaited me if I dared defy my mother-in-law's rules. But the pangs of hunger pushed me forward, outweighing my fear. I opened the fridge door deeply, anxiety washing over me.

A flicker of movement caught my eye as I scanned the fridge's contents. My heart skipped a beat as I realised my mother-in-law had spotted me. Her face contorted with anger, and a piercing scream escaped her lips, shattering the silence of the evening. The fear inside me intensified, threatening to consume my very being.

At that moment, something within me snapped. The frustration, helplessness, and years of silent submission erupted like a volcano. It was the first time since my marriage that I found the courage to speak up and defend myself. Words tumbled out of my mouth, a mixture of anger and defiance that surprised even me.

The reaction was swift and brutal. Enraged by my outburst, my husband raised his hand and delivered a stinging slap across my face. Pain exploded physically and emotionally as I crumpled to the floor, stunned and broken. He lifted me, a twisted semblance of concern on his face, and we retreated to our room.

In that room, where love and intimacy should have resided, it became a space tainted by power dynamics and control. I had no agency, no voice. I was nothing more than an object, a vessel for his desires. My mind was clouded with a devastating realisation as he forced himself upon me. I had only two choices; two paths lay before me.

The first choice was to endure, accept my fate and find solace in the physical act. But deep down, I knew it would only perpetuate the cycle of pain and submission. The second choice loomed over me, dark and terrifying. It was a desperate act of defiance, a way to reclaim my autonomy, no matter how tragic.

With a heavy heart and trembling hands, I chose the second path. In that moment of desolation, I reached for the poison, hoping to escape the suffocating grip of my circumstances. It was a choice born out of despair, a tragic consequence of a life trapped within the confines of societal expectations and abuse.

1

Enduring Shadows: The Judge, the Audience, and the Reluctant Bride

Kumudh sat nervously in the cosy armchair, her fingers tracing the edges of her saree. She had hesitated to share her story with anyone, but something about my compassionate gaze (the author Ankit) sitting across from her made her feel understood. The room was a quaint study adorned with bookshelves reaching towards the high ceiling, filled with tales from every corner of the world.

Sunlight streamed through the curtains, casting a warm glow on the wooden floor. A vintage writing desk stood in the corner, adorned with a MacBook and scattered sheets of paper. The room was a sanctuary of creativity, a space where imagination found its voice.

As Kumudh began her tale, my (the author's) eyes drifted to a large painting that hung on the wall. This depicted a vibrant portrait of Prime Minister Narendra Modi, his charismatic smile captured in intricate brushstrokes. The picture emanated a sense of pride and hope, symbolising the country's resilience and progress.

Next to the painting, a small shelf displayed various trinkets and memorabilia. Kumudh's eyes wandered to a delicate porcelain doll dressed in traditional Indian attire.

Dressed in a flowing emerald green saree, Kumudh exuded grace and strength. The saree, intricately woven with golden threads, captured the essence of her journey. Each fold of the fabric held a story, representing the twists and turns of her life that had brought her to this moment.

Her ebony hair cascaded down her shoulders, held back by a single jasmine flower tucked behind her ear. The flower's delicate fragrance filled the room. Kumudh's eyes, deep and combined with pain and resilience, mirrored the depths of her soul. They held a glimmer of hope, a determination to overcome the hurdles life had thrown her way.

The faintest hint of a smile graced her lips, hinting at the resilience she had discovered amidst the storms. Scars of past battles, both visible and hidden, adorned her caramel-toned skin, a testament to her strength and the struggles she had fought.

The air was heavy with anticipation as she prepared herself to share the story that had been etched into the deepest corners of her heart. Across from her, I am sitting (the author), a seasoned wordsmith with a pen poised above a blank sheet of paper, ready to transcribe her tale.

With a hesitant yet determined voice, Kumudh began, "I've carried this story within me for far too long, and I believe it's time to set it free. It's a story of love, loss, and the extraordinary journey that brought me to this moment."

The room seemed to hold its breath as if it, too, yearned to hear the secrets that Kumudh was about to unveil. She took a deep breath, her eyes shining with vulnerability and resilience. In that instant, she entrusted me (the author) with her most intimate thoughts and experiences, hoping I could capture the essence of her remarkable journey.

"I was born in a small town, Mhow, the birthplace of Dr Ambedkar," she continued, her voice laced with nostalgia. "Life was simple, yet filled with an inexplicable sense of magic. I discovered my insatiable curiosity for the world beyond within those rustic surroundings."

I (the author), captivated by Kumudh's presence, watched intently as her tale unfolded. I realised the weight of my responsibility—to transcribe her words and convey the depth of her emotions and the authenticity of her experiences.

Kumudh's voice gained strength as she delved deeper into her narrative.

Now fully immersed in Kumudh's world, I eagerly scribbled notes, striving to capture every nuance and emotion from her lips. It was as if her story had taken on a life of its own, demanding to be shared with the world.

My pen moved furiously across the paper, racing to keep up with Kumudh's compelling tale. Her words resonated deeply, stirring a whirlwind of emotions I knew would translate into a truly extraordinary story.

As the room filled with emotion, Kumudh concluded, her voice filled with hope and longing, "And so, dear author, now you tell me what fascinates you more about writing about my memoir and when and where you find me.

I leaned back in my chair, reminiscing about the first time I saw her. It had been an ordinary day, filled with the usual hustle and bustle of a crowded city street. Lost in my thoughts, I was drawn to a sudden burst of colour amidst the monotonous attire.

As I turned the corner, you were like a radiant jewel amidst the dull urban backdrop. You stood with an air of quiet confidence, your turquoise dress standing out amidst the muted tones of the surroundings. The vibrant hue mirrors her spirit, captivating my attention instantaneously.

Your eyes, framed by long, dark lashes, sparkled with determination and vulnerability. At that moment, our gazes briefly met, and I felt an inexplicable connection as if fate had conspired to bring us together. I was captivated by how you carried yourself and seemed to possess an untold story waiting to be unveiled.

From that very instant, I knew there was something extraordinary about you. I was drawn to your enigmatic aura, the stories that seemed to linger in the depths of your eyes. The sight of you had ignited a creative spark within me, a deep curiosity to uncover the layers of your experiences and translate them into the written word.

I couldn't help but marvel at the serendipity that had brought us together. It was as if our meeting had been written in the stars, our destinies intertwined to create a powerful narrative that would resonate with readers far and wide.

Present Day

Then I saw you carrying a tiny blue bindi that perfectly matched your sky blue and white salwar kameez. If such a possibility exists, you looked like Kareena Kapoor's more brilliant cousin." I complimented with a flirtatious smile, trying to capture Kumudh's attention.

"You have been my crush for the last few months," I confessed to Kumudh. "I've been following you everywhere, from the Ganesh temple to the doctor's clinic."

"Kumudh blushed and looked away, pretending to be uninterested. "Crush... ... What the fuck..." Kumudh responded aggressively, clearly surprised by my admission. "I'm roughly ten years older than you."

"But age is just a number, Kumudh. It doesn't define the connection between two souls," I replied, leaning closer. "Okay, I like you," as Arjun likes Malaika. I persisted, undeterred. "You're not just beautiful; you're hot and sexy too. Your features are perfect—eyes, nose, lips, and ears, all in the right size and place. That's what makes a girl truly beautiful. And nowadays, we boys appreciate the masterpiece."

Kumudh raised an eyebrow at my bold words. "The masterpiece, huh?" she asserted, clearly intrigued.

"Yes, a masterpiece," I affirmed with a smile. "Who knows everything? All we need to show is our stamina. And on the other hand, aged women also love perseverance," I teased, enjoying our banter.

"Hmm, so silly," Kumudh articulated, trying to hide her growing smile.

"Hmm, you're quite something," she mused.

"Alright, let me continue my story later. Tell me about yourself," I said, changing the subject and pretending to focus on the story.

"I have never poured my heart out regarding this, not even to my 'Maasi' and my best friends, because it brings tears to my eyes, and I don't want to feel weak. So please have patience with my story, Ankit," Kumudh said, her voice filled with vulnerability and strength.

"Okay, now back to my memoir," Kumudh resumed, wiping away a tear that had escaped her eye.

(November 2011)

"I have many proposals for the wedding," Kumudh continued, her gaze distant. "I rejected all the proposals and told my family to give me more time. But one day, when my family went to a wedding, they heard something objectionable..."

I leaned closer, genuinely intrigued by her tale. "What did they hear?" I asked, unable to contain my curiosity.

"Some neighbours were posing together, and they were schmoozing about me," Kumudh revealed, a touch of bitterness in her voice. "One of them said, 'Hey, have you heard anything about Kumudh? She was in love with a boy a year ago, and they came to her house with a marriage proposal, but she rejected him because now she has another one. They came to her house. I saw them with my own eyes. Nowadays, girls are not caring for their parents...' she recounted, her voice trembling with emotion.

I reached out and gently placed my hand on hers, offering support. "I'm sorry you had to go through that. It must have been incredibly tough," I said, my tone sincere.

Kumudh nodded, her eyes moist with unshed tears. "After listening to these shits, my family members were astounded... They got freaked out entirely. And after that occurrence, even though I was not sinful, that made me endure..."

I squeezed her hand gently, trying to comfort her. "You're strong, Kumudh. And sometimes, enduring difficult moments can reveal our true strength," I reassured her.

"After this occurrence, my family started pressuring me to get married. And for this, they have called a family, which our relatives insinuate," Kumudh continued, her voice filled with resignation.

(November 30, 2011)

"A family from Mumbai came to see me for the wedding," Kumudh revealed. "I felt despondent throughout; my uncle, 'Maasi,' and my maternal grandmother were discussing with the groom's family."

"As I waited in my room, I felt like a prisoner," she continued, her voice filled with resignation and sadness.

"Even my face looks like I haven't slept for months. I have worn a lehenga choli, and my waistline is also witnessing the guy. I entered the drawing room and brushed a strand of my hair behind my ear," she continued, her voice filled with fear and resignation. As I entered the room, I felt like a prisoner facing a judge and an audience waiting for the verdict."

"There were about 10-11 people," Kumudh recalled, a touch of bitterness in her voice. "The judge and audience were bribed with tea and snacks. I glanced at the boy who had come to see me and noticed he had a dark complexion.

'What the fuck ' I said to myself, 'he's so brunette, even my vagina is brighter than him.'"

Despite her reservations, I didn't say anything to my Nani and quietly nodded in agreement for the match. The boy's name was Ajay Somani, and the families decided on a wedding date—January 16, 2012.

"I wanted more time to escape from the darkness," Kumudh confessed, her voice tinged with regret. "But my family had already chosen the date. So, I didn't say anything to them and reluctantly prepared for the earlier wedding date."

As Kumudh finished her tale, there was a momentary silence between us. The weight of her experiences hung in the air, and I couldn't help but feel a deep sense of empathy and admiration for her resilience.

2

Lotus in a Co-Ed Garden

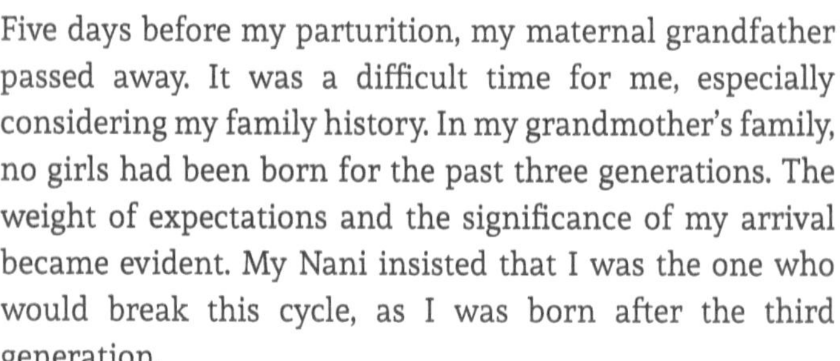

Five days before my parturition, my maternal grandfather passed away. It was a difficult time for me, especially considering my family history. In my grandmother's family, no girls had been born for the past three generations. The weight of expectations and the significance of my arrival became evident. My Nani insisted that I was the one who would break this cycle, as I was born after the third generation.

Amidst this backdrop, my Nani courageously decided to keep me despite the conflicts it caused between my grandmother's family and hers. Then, she named me "Kumudh," meaning lotus, a symbol of beauty and purity that she hoped would guide me through life.

Being raised in my Nani's family meant I spent little time with my parents. Instead, my "Maasi" became my best friend and confidante during my childhood. I was diligent and meticulous when she was around, but everything changed when she married. I became more reserved and guarded.

Living in a small town, I found solace in the protection of my shell. I never ventured out with friends, and the thought of interacting with boys was inconceivable. In the 12th standard, I had no friends, and no one seemed to like me. However, after completing my 12th grade, a transformation took place within me.

Suddenly, I felt my body changing, evolving into a womanly figure. By 18, my chest had developed into a 32-inch breast. I still vividly remember the excitement and sense of womanhood when I bought my first bra at 15. It was as if I wanted the entire universe to know that I was embracing this new phase of my life.

My desire to attend an all-girls college stemmed from my deep-rooted fear and apprehension towards boys. Having spent my life in a girls' school, the thought of being in a co-ed environment terrified me. However, my uncle, who had a different perspective, insisted I join a co-ed college.

I had to complete all the admission forms and other formalities alone since I had no friends to rely on. This began a significant twist in my life that would completely transform my perspective.

And then came the first day of college, a pivotal moment. I wore a blue denim outfit with a casual top and a hijab with my long, dark hair flowing down to my waist. As I entered the class, all eyes were on me, and I could sense their astonishment as if I had walked in wearing a bikini.

I attended college regularly, maintaining my disciplined and determined nature, even though I did not understand what a penis looked like.

I was alone in college for the initial two months, with no friends to rely on. However, slowly, more girls started coming regularly, and I began to form connections. I found solace in the company of a group of five to six girls. With time, my interest in attending college grew, and I genuinely enjoyed the college life I once feared.

Surprisingly, I started gaining popularity in college, becoming known as a regular and dedicated student. Teachers began to appreciate my efforts and commitment. But, as life would have it, things took an unexpected turn.

Our group of girls decided to call ourselves the "Holy Devils." We developed strong bonds within this group, and two boys, Ridhaan and Ojas, became an integral part of it.

Ridhaan is a tall and athletic young man with a charming smile that lights up his face. He has a lean yet muscular build, owing to his dedication to regular workouts and sports activities. His jet-black hair is neatly styled, adding to his overall bright appearance. Ridhaan has striking hazel eyes seem to hold a mischievous glint, often reflecting his playful nature. His warm, caramel-toned skin complements his features, giving him a radiant and friendly aura.

On the other hand, Ojas is slightly shorter in height than Ridhaan, but his infectious energy and cheerful personality make him stand out from any crowd. His lean and wiry build suggests his fondness for outdoor adventures and physical activities. Ojas's sandy-brown hair is styled carefree, with a few locks falling casually over his forehead. His bright, expressive eyes, the colour of deep blue oceans, twinkle with enthusiasm and curiosity. Ojas's fair complexion has a healthy glow, reflecting his active lifestyle and love for outdoor sports.

Despite my initial reservations, I found myself bonding with them. I also had a best friend, Riya, who is the epitome of a free spirit. She's vibrant, spontaneous, and full of energy. She possesses an infectious enthusiasm for life and is always up for an adventure. Riya has a magnetic personality that draws people towards her. She's empathetic, understanding, and a great listener. Her loyalty and dedication to her friends are unmatched, making her the perfect confidante. She was like my sister.

Riya, Ridhaan, and Ojas developed a fondness for the tea I made, and they would often visit my home to enjoy it. We cherished our college life and graduation, relishing every moment. However, amidst all the joy, it became apparent that Riya had developed feelings for Ridhaan. Although it was evident to everyone in our group, she hadn't expressed her emotions to any of us.

3

Raindrops and Culinary Delights: Unveiling Mandav's Treasures

Our graduation was completed, and the four of us—Riya, Ridhaan, Ojas, and I—had become incredibly close. We decided to enrol in the same college and head to DAVV Indore to obtain our master's degrees.

Three years had passed since we became friends, and now we were in our fourth year of college. We are planning a trip to celebrate this milestone.

Hey everyone, I've been planning a trip to Mandav on August 25th, 2009. I've heard it has stunning historical monuments and breathtaking views. What do you all think?

Riya: That sounds amazing, Kumudh! I'm up for it. I've always wanted to visit Mandav. Plus, I've heard they have this stunning fort that overlooks the entire city. It's like something out of a fairytale.

Ridhaan: Mandav? Count me in! I've been wanting to go there for ages. I heard about this picturesque lake called Roopmati's Lake, and the sunset views are supposed to be breathtaking.

Ojas: Mandav it is then! I've heard the food there is delicious. I can't wait to try the local cuisine. And hey, it'll be the perfect opportunity to take some fantastic pictures.

Kumudh: Great! It's settled, then. We'll plan a weekend trip to Mandav. But hey, let's play a little game while we're at it. Let's each devise the funniest, most embarrassing travel story we can imagine. Whoever has the best story gets a treat from the rest of us.

Riya: Oh, I'm so excited about that! I've got one from a trip I took with my family. We were on a road trip, and I got carsick while driving through a mountainous region. It was a very colourful experience, and I had to make several unplanned pit stops. It was so embarrassing!

Ridhaan: Haha, that's hilarious, Riya! I once went hiking with some friends, and we decided to go off the beaten path. We got lost in the woods for hours, and I accidentally fell into a muddy puddle. I was covered in mud from head to toe, and my friends couldn't stop laughing at me.

Ojas: Oh, man! That must have been quite the sight, Ridhaan. My embarrassing travel story involves trying to impress a cute girl during a beach vacation. I thought I'd show off my surfing skills, but instead, I wiped out spectacularly in front of everyone. I swallowed so much seawater, and my hair was a mess. Needless to say, the girl wasn't too, could have been more.

Kumudh: Haha, these stories are gold! Okay, here's mine. I decided to try out a local dance performance on a previous trip. I could impress everyone with my moves, but I tripped on my feet and accidentally knocked over one of the performers. It was like a domino effect, and the performance came to a screeching halt. I felt so embarrassed!

Riya: Kumudh, that's just too funny! I can't wait to hear more stories like these during our trip. It's going to be a laughter-filled adventure. Let's ensure we capture all these moments and create memories that'll last a lifetime.

Ridhaan: Absolutely, Riya! Our trip to Mandav is going to be legendary. We'll explore the beautiful sights, enjoy delicious food, and have a ton of laughs along the way. I can't wait to see what kind of hilarious mishaps and unforgettable moments we'll experience together.

Ojas: I'm already looking forward to the fantastic pictures we'll take and the stories we'll share with everyone. This trip will be epic, and we'll return with enough tales to entertain us for years.

Mandav, here we come.

The next day.

I got pledged," I added disappointedly. "I won't be able to come with you guys on this trip. You three should go and enjoy."

"Okay, if you're not coming, we might as well cancel the trip," Ridhaan replied.

Ridhaan's response took me aback. Maybe he was looking out for me as a friend, so I brushed it off and took it lightly. Little did I know that this moment would change my life.

My friends pleaded with me to come along, leaving me with no choice but to join them. "I'm coming with you guys," I finally said, and Ridhaan seemed genuinely pleased to hear this.

August 25th 2009

As we made our way to Mandav, we were greeted by the town's enchanting beauty. The rain had just begun to fall, adding a touch of magic to the atmosphere.

Kumudh: Wow, look at the lush greenery surrounding us! The rain has breathed life into every tree and blade of grass, making the colours more vibrant.

Riya: Absolutely! And the raindrops glistening on the leaves and petals create a mesmerising sight. It's like nature itself is adorned with sparkling diamonds. The scent of wet earth and flowers fills the air, adding a hint of romance to our adventure.

Ridhaan: And let's remember the architecture! Mandav is famous for its historical monuments, which look even more majestic in this rain. The ancient fort stands tall, its walls glistening with moisture. The soft, diffused light accentuates the intricate carvings and grand archways. It's like stepping into a different era.

Ojas: I couldn't agree more, Ridhaan. And look at the surroundings—the rolling hills, the meandering rivers. The rain has turned everything into a painting. The mist adds an ethereal touch, shrouding the landscape in a mysterious charm. I can't wait to capture these moments with my camera.

Kumudh: As we explore Mandav, we'll witness the rain's gentle touch on the town's hidden treasures. Like Rani Roopmati's Pavilion, the step wells glisten with rainwater, reflecting the sky above. It's as if the heavens have blessed these structures with their tears.

Riya: And let's remember the people of Mandav. Even in the rain, their warmth and hospitality shine through. The locals go about their daily lives, embracing the shower with joy. The laughter and cheerful conversations add to the tapestry of sounds that fills the air.

Ridhaan: Absolutely, Riya. And as night falls, the rain transforms Mandav into a magical wonderland. The illuminated structures, the sound of raindrops hitting the rooftops, and the cosy cafes inviting us to take shelter—it's like a scene from a fairytale.

Ojas: Our trip to Mandav couldn't have been timed more perfectly. The rain has breathed new life into this place, enhancing its beauty and charm. We are truly fortunate to witness the union of nature and history in such a breathtaking setting.

Kumudh: Indeed, Ojas. As the rain continues to fall, let's embrace every moment, immerse ourselves in the beauty of Mandav, and create memories that will forever be etched in our hearts.

With broad smiles, we four ventured further into Mandav, ready to experience the beauty and enchantment of the rain-soaked town.

I was thoroughly enjoying myself in the rain. My dress was drenched, and even my balconette bra seemed to be feeling the water. I discreetly used my scarf to cover up.

The rain had subsided, leaving a relaxed and refreshing atmosphere in Mandav. After exploring all the forts and indulging in Mandav's beauty, we found a picturesque bench overlooking a stunning view. We couldn't resist sitting and taking in the beauty around us.

Ridhaan and Ojas decided to check out a nearby restaurant, leaving Riya and me.

The sound of raindrops falling on the leaves created a soothing rhythm as they sat down, feeling the coolness of the wet wooden bench beneath them. The ambience was perfect for a heartfelt conversation.

Riya: (sighs) Kumudh, I must tell you something. It's been weighing on my heart for a while now.

What is it, Riya? You know you can share anything with me. I'm here for you. "I voiced my concern," I declared.

Riya: (pauses momentarily, gathering her thoughts) Kumudh, I think... no, I know I have feelings for Ridhaan. It's been growing stronger daily, and I can't keep it to myself anymore.

Riya, something like this might be on your mind. And you know what? It's okay. Love is beautiful, and feeling that way about someone is natural. Ridhaan is a great guy, and I'm sure he'll appreciate your honesty."I said with a gentle smile."

Riya: (nervously) I hope so, Kumudh. But what if he doesn't feel the same way? What if it ruins our friendship?

I just wanted to tell you something about Ridhaan. He's a caring and understanding person. Even if he doesn't have the same romantic feelings for you, he'll handle it gracefully and kindly. Your friendship is strong, and it can weather any storm. I expressed

Riya: (finding comfort in Kumudh's words) Thank you, Kumudh. Your support means the world to me. I just needed to confide in someone, and I'm glad it's you.

You don't have to thank me, Riya. That's what friends are for. I'm here to listen, support, and stand by your side through thick and thin. And who knows, maybe Ridhaan feels the same way about you. Love has a funny way of surprising us.

Riya: (smiling, a glimmer of hope in her eyes) I hope so, Kumudh. I can't deny these feelings anymore. It's time to leap of faith and see where it leads for Ojas and me, as he likes you.

I chuckled and replied, "Yeah, I'm aware of that. But I only see Ojas as my best friend.".

Just as we continued our conversation, Ridhaan and Ojas returned, their faces lit up with excitement.

Hey, guys! We found a fantastic local restaurant just a few streets away. The aroma of the food is irresistible, Ridhaan expressed

You won't believe the variety of dishes they offer. It's a food lover's paradise. We can't wait to dig in! Ojas said, his mouth watering.

Perfect timing, you two. Riya and I were having a heart-to-heart.

Riya: (blushing slightly) We had much to catch up on. But now, let's indulge in some delicious food and create even more memories in Mandav.

With laughter and anticipation in their hearts, we made our way to the restaurant.

We sat around a wooden table in a cosy local restaurant in Mandav. The aroma of freshly prepared food filled the air, whetting our appetites. We had just ordered a popular Rajasthani delicacy, dal baati, and awaited its arrival.

Riya: (rubbing her hands together) I can't wait to try the dal baati here. I've heard it's delicious. The combination of the flavorful lentil curry and the crispy baati sounds divine.

Riya. Rajasthani cuisine is known for its rich flavours and unique preparations. Dal baati is one of the cuisine's gems. I'm excited to see how it tastes in Mandav. "Tum sochogi kyon itna main tumse pyaar karoon" .I made a statement while the background song murmured.

Ridhaan: (nodding) Me too. I've been looking forward to this ever since we planned this trip. I heard the baatis here are perfectly cooked, with a crispy exterior and a soft, fluffy interior. And when paired with the aromatic dal, it's a match made in culinary heaven.

Ojas: (admiring the ambience) The restaurant adds to the experience. The rustic decor and soft '90s music make us feel like we've entered a different era. And now, we get to indulge in this local delight.

"Dewaanon ki ye baatein, deewane jaante hain
Jalne mein kya mazaa hai, parwaane jaante hain
Tum yunhi jalate rehna, aa-aakar khwabon mein"

As we were going to break the restaurant's mirrors with our voices, the waiter approached our table, carrying sizzling platters of dal baati. The golden-brown baatis were beautifully arranged, accompanied by two bowls of piping hot dal and an array of chutneys and pickles.

Waiter: (with a warm smile) Here's your order of dal baati, freshly prepared and straight from our kitchen. Enjoy!

We eagerly dug in, our taste buds dancing joyfully as we savoured each bite. The crispy texture of the baatis combined with the creamy dal created a symphony of flavours in their mouths.

Oh my goodness, this is amazing! The baati melts in your mouth, and the dal has a depth of flavour. It's like a party for my taste buds. Said Riya: (closing her eyes, savouring the taste)

I couldn't have described it better, Riya. The blend of spices in the dal is perfect, and the baatis are a delight. It's no wonder this dish is so prevalent in Rajasthan. I said while nodding in agreement.

Here's to discovering the culinary gems of Mandav. Cheers! Said Ojas (raising his glass of buttermilk)

We clinked our glasses together, toasting our friendship, the delicious food, and the beautiful memories we were creating on our trip. As we continued our meal, laughter and joy filled the air, weaving a tapestry of unforgettable moments.

While we were having a good time, I noticed that Ridhaan appeared lost in thought.

It seemed like he was planning something special.

The thought crossed my mind that Ridhaan might be planning to propose to Riya.

Oh, how wrong I was...

4

Shadows of Solitude: Desires Unveiled

April 24, 2011

The house was excited as my maternal uncle and aunt celebrated their anniversary. The living room was adorned with colourful decorations, and the aroma of delicious food wafted through the air. Laughter and cheerful conversations filled every corner, but I felt detached from the festivities.

I sat alone in my room, the weight of depression weighing heavily on my shoulders. The sound of muffled laughter and joyful voices seeped through the closed door, a stark reminder of the happiness I couldn't grasp. With a heavy sigh, I turned on the air conditioner to create a cocoon of solitude.

I removed my outfit, and my mind drifted aimlessly, caught in the abyss of my thoughts. I stood there in lingerie, feeling vulnerable and lost. The room felt suffocating, and the silence was deafening. I turned to an English movie to escape my despair, hoping it would distract my troubled mind. As the scenes unfolded, I felt a peculiar sensation between my legs, a physical response to the provocative imagery. My body reacted, becoming wet and aroused. This involuntary reaction confused me more, adding to my internal turmoil. Overwhelmed by the conflicting emotions, I surrendered to my body's desires, seeking a temporary escape from my depressive state. I removed the sheet covering me, exposing myself to the empty room.

Just imagine a charming fair girl who is in depression and who even don't know what the fuck she is doing is rubbing her Vagina covered with big hairs.

Wow... I, Ankit, mooned...

Hmmm... dick-raising encounter for the readers,

"I am sure," Kumudh said, becoming shy.

It was a raw and intimate moment that manifested her pain and longing. The act was a desperate attempt to find solace, to feel something amidst the numbness that consumed her.

5
The Distant Drumbeats of Destiny

15th January 2012

We all had landed in the city of camels, Rajasthan, for my destined wedding.

As the family stepped out of the vehicle, we were greeted by the warm breeze of Rajasthan. The air carried the scent of spices and a hint of excitement.

"Wow, look at this place!" exclaimed Maasi, her jaw dropping as he took in the ornate architecture and vibrant colours adorning the hotel. "I've never seen anything quite like it!"

Shruti (my sister) gasped, her eyes sparkling with awe. "The decorations are breathtaking! It feels like we've stepped into a royal palace."

The rest of the family stood beside me, mesmerised by the intricate designs and rich cultural details that adorned every hotel corner. The walls were decorated with hand-painted murals depicting Rajasthani folk tales, and the corridors were lined with colourful tapestries and shimmering chandeliers.

As we entered the lobby, we were greeted by the warm smiles of the hotel staff dressed in traditional Rajasthani attire. The reception area was adorned with fragrant flowers and garlands, their sweet aroma filling the air.

"This is incredible," whispered Nani, her voice filled with astonishment. "I can't believe how they've captured the essence of Rajasthan in every little detail."

Maa nodded in agreement, her eyes twinkling with delight.

The family continued to explore the hotel, finding each room more exquisite than the last. The dining hall was adorned with colourful Rajasthani paintings, and the tables were set with fine silverware and vibrant Rajasthani tablecloths. The aroma of freshly prepared Rajasthani delicacies wafted through the air, making their mouths water.

"Is this heaven?" whispered Shruti, her eyes wide with wonder. "Everything is so beautiful and fancy!"

Maa laughed, ruffling Shruti's hair. "Well, it sure feels like it. But remember, we're here to enjoy and make the most of this wonderful experience together."

Dad grinned, a mischievous twinkle in his eyes. "And that includes indulging in all the delicious Rajasthani food he can access!"

Laughter filled the air as the family walked through the hotel, marvelling at the beauty and culture surrounding them. They knew their time in Rajasthan would be an adventure filled with unforgettable memories, and they were sad that I would no longer be staying with them.

As they settled into their rooms, the anticipation for the days ahead grew.

In a room adorned with colourful decorations and lively music playing in the background, Maa, Maasi, and Nani were excitedly preparing for the upcoming Mahila Sangeet ritual. The air was filled with laughter and the clinking of bangles as they busily arranged flowers, set up the stage, and rehearsed their dance steps.

Meanwhile, I was alone in my room, lost in my thoughts. My mind drifted to thoughts of my new family, wondering how they would accept me and whether I would find the love and understanding I had always longed for.

I found myself contemplating my new family, wondering what they would be like and how they would accept me into their lives. Would they be welcoming and warm or distant and reserved? Would they understand my quirks and idiosyncrasies, or would I have to adapt to fit into their mould?

I imagined myself stepping into a world unknown, where I would have to navigate the intricacies of new relationships, customs, and traditions. Can I meet their expectations and make a place for myself in their natures?

A mix of hope and apprehension coursed through my veins. I yearned for a loving and supportive family, eager to embrace me with open arms.

As I stared blankly at my reflection in the mirror, Maasi entered the room, her face beaming with excitement. She sat beside me and gently placed a hand on my shoulder.

"Kumudh, what's bothering you?" she asked, concern evident in her voice.

I sighed deeply, my eyes welling up with tears.

Maasi took my hand and squeezed it reassuringly. "I understand your fears, Kumudh, but remember, our family has chosen this path for you with love and the hope of a better future. Your happiness is important to all of us, and we'll support you every step of the way."

Just then, Maa and Nani entered the room, their eyes filled with affection and understanding. They knew that Kumudh's journey was arduous and wanted to give me the love and encouragement I needed.

"Life is a series of unknowns, my child. Embrace this new chapter with an open heart, and remember that you carry the love and values of our family within you. You are never alone." Nani said, her eyes twinkling with wisdom.

Now get ready (They leave).

However, amidst these thoughts, I couldn't help but reminisce about that guy who had left me at such a critical point in my life. I still dreamt of intimate moments with him, longing for his touch and presence. But those fantasies were now futile. From tomorrow onwards, everything will be about Ajay Somani, my husband. I resolved that I wouldn't indulge in certain acts with him, drawing boundaries for myself.

As I pondered these bittersweet memories, my "Maasi" entered my room again and said, "Kumudh, you're not ready yet! The groom's family has arrived."

16th January, 2012
(My wedding day)

I was overwhelmed with concern about Ajay's family. They had displayed such appalling behaviour during last night's program. I was infuriated with myself for agreeing to marry this guy. I worried about what my life would be like starting from tomorrow. However, at this point, there was nothing I could do. This was my fate.

**

"Kumudh, it's 6:30 PM, and you're not ready yet. Come on, hurry up,"

Maasi, dressed in an elegant saree, entered the room with urgency. She glanced at the clock and then turned her attention to me; I was having my hair styled. "Kumudh, my dear, we don't have much time left. The groom can reach here anytime. We need to make sure you're ready," she said, her voice filled with concern and excitement.

The hairdresser worked quickly, weaving intricate braids adorned with delicate flowers. The makeup artist gently applied layers of makeup, highlighting my natural beauty. Maasi watched with anticipation, her hands nervously fidgeting with my dress. "We have to make sure you look perfect, my darling.

As the final touches were added, Maasi rechecked the watch. "The baraat will be here any moment. We need to ensure everything is in place," she exclaimed, trying to hide the excitement and anticipation in her voice.

Maasi softened, a proud smile gracing my face. "You're going to be the most beautiful bride, my dear. Remember, this day marks the beginning of a new chapter in your life. Enjoy every moment," she said, her voice filled with a mother's love and warmth.

The room became momentarily calm as Maasi and the bridal party gathered around me, appreciating the transformation. There was an unspoken understanding that time was of the essence, and every moment counted.

With a final glance in the mirror, I nodded to Maasi, signifying I was ready. Maasi's eyes sparkled with pride and love as she took my hand. "It's time, my dear. Let's go and start this beautiful journey together," she said, her voice steady and filled with anticipation.

The door creaked open, and Maa and Nani walked in.

Maa's eyes were filled with tears as she looked at me, her girl grown up and ready to start a new chapter in her life. She approached me, her hands trembling, and gently brushed away a stray tear from my cheek. "My dear, my beautiful Kumudh, today is your special day," she whispered, her voice full of emotion.

Maasi, "Oh, Kumudh! Look at this lehenga! It's fit for a queen," she exclaimed, her eyes twinkling with excitement. "Kumudh, my dear, you look stunning! Like a Bollywood diva," Maasi exclaimed, her voice filled with excitement and admiration. "You remind me of Kareena Kapoor herself, a true epitome of grace and charm."

Nani, the wise matriarch of the family, entered the room with a serene smile. Her presence brought a sense of calm and reassurance. She approached me and placed a gentle hand on my shoulder.

As they left the room, I stood before the mirror, adorned in the breathtaking lehenga. A flood of emotions washed over me. Amidst the excitement and joy, her thoughts wandered to a painful memory—the mother fucker boy's memory.

Amid the celebrations, I couldn't help but recall my heartache. The promises broken, the dreams shattered—it was a wound that had yet to heal fully. My heart felt heavy with the weight of that past pain, even as I embarked on a new chapter of my life.

A mix of anger, sadness, and confusion swirled within me. I wondered why I still carried the burden of those memories, why my ex's betrayal lingered in my thoughts on such a momentous day. It felt like a cruel twist of fate, a haunting reminder of the past.

ᢥᢥᢥ

In the dimly lit room, I sat on the edge of my bed, nervously twirling my fingers as I anxiously awaited the arrival of the baraat—the groom's procession. My mind was clouded with emotions, and uncertainty washed over me.

As the minutes ticked by, a small part of me wished for the baraat never to arrive. It was a fleeting thought, born out of the fear of the unknown and the weight of my past experiences.

In the silence of the room, I allowed myself a moment of vulnerability, contemplating the significance of this day. Doubts and questions raced through my mind. Would this marriage bring me love, happiness, and companionship? Or would it be another chapter of my life filled with compromise and unfulfilled dreams?

*****

Now it's 12:03:53 AM; I remember the exact time because my hell procession has reported on this time.

The distant sound of drums and "Bahaaron phool barasaao."

Shouts grew louder, signalling the arrival of the baraat. My heart skipped a beat as anticipation filled the room. I stood near the window, peering outside, watching the procession draw closer with every passing second.

As the baraat entered the wedding venue, vibrant colours and exuberant energy filled the air. The groom's family and friends danced in jubilation, their footsteps resonating with the beats of the dhol. The atmosphere was alive with laughter, music, and the unmistakable joy of celebration.

But amidst the grandeur and excitement, a mix of emotions swirled within me. I couldn't help but wonder what lay beyond the festivity—whether this union would bring happiness and fulfilment or become a mere façade of marital bliss.

My eyes wandered to the groom, dressed in traditional attire, riding a beautifully adorned horse. He looked like a Bandwala.

The vibrant beats of the dhol reverberated through the air as the time for me to approach the groom. My family, adorned in traditional attire, gathered around me, their eyes filled with love and excitement. They formed a protective circle, ready to escort me for the auspicious ritual.

PAPA, dressed in a regal sherwani, walked beside me, holding my hand with pride and affection. MA and Maasi, adorned in an elegant saree, walked on the other side, my eyes brimming with joy, nostalgia, and bittersweetness. The rest of the family, including her siblings, aunts, and uncles, surrounded her, creating a cocoon of support and love.

As I entered the venue, all eyes turned towards me, captivated by my stunning appearance. I wore a pink and purple coloured bridal dress, a vision of beauty and elegance. The dress flowed gracefully, hugging my figure in all the right places.

The dress's bodice was adorned with intricate embroidery and delicate patterns of flowers and vines that seemed to dance across the fabric. Sparkling sequins and shimmering beads added a touch of glamour, catching the light with every movement.

The dress transitioned seamlessly into a voluminous skirt cascading to the floor. Layers of soft tulle created a romantic and ethereal effect, billowing with every step I took. The pink and purple hues blended in a harmonious gradient, creating a captivating visual display.

The dress train trailed behind me as I walked, creating a regal aura. The intricate embroidery continued along the hemline, adding a touch of opulence to the already breathtaking ensemble.

As she stood there, a vision of love and beauty, everyone in the room was in awe of the bride's appearance. The pink and purple coloured bridal dress perfectly captured her essence, showcasing her individuality and style. She exuded confidence and happiness, ready to embark on this new chapter of her life with grace and poise.

*****

We reached the hall, which was adorned with colourful flowers and shimmering lights, glowing warmly for the eagerly awaiting guests. The moment had arrived for the garland ceremony, where I, the bride, would exchange garlands with the groom, Ajay Somani. I stood on one side of the beautifully decorated place, my heart pounding with nervousness and apprehension.

As the groom, dressed in traditional attire, approached the stage, worry washed over me. My mind raced with thoughts of his appearance, and I couldn't shake the feeling of uncertainty. What if our physical mismatch overshadowed the celebration? What would the guests think?

I briefly scanned the crowd, noticing the curious gazes fixed upon me. The guests whispered amongst themselves, captivated by my resplendent beauty.

As the groom climbed the steps, Is this your groom?

What the fuck?

The moment arrived—the exchange of garlands. I took a deep breath, trembling hands clutching the vibrant floral garland. As our eyes met, a flicker of uncertainty crossed my mind.

I lifted the garland and placed it around the groom's (Ajay) neck, sealing the ceremony with hope and apprehension.

I had earlier decided to tease my groom when my marriage occurred, and this tradition continues. But now, all my dreams are useless; I bow my neck and wear the garland.

The guests erupted into applause and cheers, their focus shifting from the groom to the radiant bride standing before them.

As the celebrations continued, my heart swelled with gratitude for the support and love I received from her family and friends. She vowed to make this marriage a journey of growth, finding solace in the belief that true beauty resided within their connection—a connection that would unfold with time, nurturing the seeds of love and understanding.

*****

The Mama Phera, a significant Marwadi tradition, was about to occur. My heart raced with a mix of excitement and anticipation. It symbolised the bond between my maternal uncle (Mama) and me—a glue essential in Marwadi culture.

The guests gathered around, their eyes fixed on the couple. The room buzzed with anticipation as the priest began to recite sacred chants, invoking the blessings of the divine. Mama, dressed in traditional attire, approached me and Ajay with a beaming smile.

As Mama walked towards us, I couldn't help but feel a surge of affection and gratitude. He had been a pillar of support throughout my life, always there to offer guidance and love. I cherished their bond, and Mama Phera held a special place in her heart.

Ajay is in the middle; MAMA put my hand in his and took three circumambulations, covering the groom.

My worries and anxieties began to dissipate with each step he took. I focused on the love and warmth radiating from her Mama, feeling blessed to have him by my side on this joyous occasion. Mama's presence brought comfort and reassurance, reminding me that I was entering a new phase of life with the blessings and support of my entire family.

As Mama reached us, he extended his arms, offering blessings and guidance. Ajay and I respectfully bowed, seeking his blessings for a prosperous and harmonious married life. The priest continued the rituals, reciting prayers and mantras, further sanctifying the bond between the bride and groom.

Amidst the sacred chants and the heartfelt blessings, my heart swelled with gratitude and a sense of belonging. The Mama Phera reinforced the notion of family unity and the interconnectedness of generations. It represented the groom's acceptance into my family, solidifying the bond between our families.

As the ceremony concluded, the room erupted with applause and jubilant cheers. The guests showered us with blessings and good wishes, their faces lit up with joy.

At that moment, I realised that Mama Phera wasn't just a tradition—it was a testament to the love and support she had received from her Mama throughout her life. It symbolised the unbreakable bond of family and the strength it provided as she embarked on this new chapter of her life.

With a heart filled with love and anticipation, Ajay and I moved forward, ready to embrace the journey ahead, walking towards the stage.

(AFTER A FEW HOURS)

It was almost midnight now, after a grand reception. I was already exhausted from the long hours of waiting for the procession and for standing and welcoming guests, maintaining a smile that made my cheeks hurt, and posing for numerous photo sessions, which no one would remember, maybe just the young ones who would post them on Facebook with an earth-shattering caption about how great they felt and wait for likes.

Now, at 2 AM, we eat our meal, and I want to collapse on my bed. Please don't take it there; I want to sleep alone.

*****

The pandit stood at the centre of the dimly lit room, adorned with flickering candles, reciting verses that echoed with ancient wisdom. We stood side by side, our hands clasped together, hearts pounding with anticipation. The para ceremony symbolised the eternal bond we were about to forge, circling the holy fire seven times, pledging our love, loyalty, and commitment to each other.

The applause slowly faded into the background as I stood there, my heart still racing, but my mind transported to a different time and place. Memories of a love long gone began to weave into the fabric of my thoughts, intertwining with the present moment.

As the pandit's voice faded, I couldn't help but steal a glance at my soon-to-be husband. His eyes sparkled with excitement and joy, his smile radiating warmth. Yet, in that fleeting moment, I couldn't help but see a ghost of someone else. Someone who had once held my heart in his hands.

Lost in the labyrinth of my thoughts, I felt a gentle tug on my hand. My husband, now my partner for life, looked at me with concern etched across his face. "Are you alright ?" he whispered, his voice filled with tenderness.

I blinked, snapping back to the present and smiling. "Yes," I replied softly, though the word felt heavy on my lips. The weight of the past pressed upon me, threatening to engulf the joy of the present moment.

As we began to walk around the sacred fire, the atmosphere was filled with ethereal energy.

The flickering flames danced, casting an enchanting glow on my family members' faces while the soft chant of the pandit reverberated through the chamber. Each step we took felt like a milestone. My efforts felt heavier now. The flickering flames seemed to mirror the flicker of memories in my mind, casting shadows that danced across my heart.

In the corner of my eye, I noticed the photographer still capturing the intricacies of our union. His camera lens focused on our intertwined fingers, immortalising a moment that felt bittersweet to me. I wondered if he could sense the undercurrent of emotions that swirled within me, the delicate balance between the love I was embracing and the love I had left behind. As we completed the final phera, the pandit's voice echoed through the room again, filling the air with blessings and affirmations. But this time, as the words washed over me, they reminded me of my chosen path.

6

The Weight of Expectations: The Complexities of a New Life

♡

18 January 2012 (After Marriage)

"Bhiwandi," a village in Maharashtra

We arrived at my new home. I had envisioned creating a new home that would be better than my old one, but reality hit me hard.

I looked around in disbelief, noticing the peeling paint on the walls, the cracked floors, and the musty smell in the air. This was supposed to be my new beginning, a fresh start, but instead, it felt like a step backwards.

As I stood there, my mind raced with thoughts. How would I adjust to this cramped space? Would I ever feel at home here? A surge of disappointment washed over me, and I couldn't help but wonder if I had made the right decision.

I glanced at my new in-laws, who seemed unfazed by the state of the house. They greeted me warmly, their smiles masking any hint of dissatisfaction. They had accepted this as their reality, but for me, it was a stark contrast to the life I had known.

I never imagined that I would marry a guy who didn't have a proper house.

*****

"What the fuck? So, you said yes without even considering the guy. You hadn't even seen their house before marriage," I (Ankit) interjected, stopping Kumudh.

*****

"Yes," Kumudh responded.

Kumudh continued her story, "Just like how the goddess Sati reincarnated on earth as the daughter of the King of Himachal, Raja Himavat, and Queen Mena, they named her 'Parvati.' As she grew up, she lost herself, yearning for Lord Shiva.

When Parvati reached marriageable age, Narad Muni arrived at Raja Himavat's fort to meet her. Knowing that Parvati was reborn as Sati, when Raja Himavat asked Narad Muni to find a wealthy and noble king for his daughter Parvati, Narad Muni slyly mentioned the name Mahadev.

"Mahadev," the king remarked, impressed by the beautiful name.

"And is he rich or not?" the king inquired.

"There is so much wealth that even Brahma and Vishnu seek their blessings," Narad Muni replied.

Upon hearing such praises without meeting or seeing Mahadev, Raja Himavat agreed to the relationship.

The same thing happened to me. My family listened to the praises and finalised my marriage without seeing the house or other details. They even decided to organise the wedding ceremony in Rajasthan and contribute to the expenses.

I entered a house reminiscent of a shanty rather than a home. Everyone's eyes were fixed on me, judging and wanting to know how I looked without the heavy bridal makeup. Were my features fairer than my husband's, or was my makeup merely a facade? Did we look good together? These thoughts occupied their minds. Maybe it was because mine was an arranged marriage. I felt immensely embarrassed as I despised being scrutinised in every aspect—how I dressed, ate, and so on.

But here is the main point: I am not criticising my in-laws. They are good people. However, the relatives and acquaintances associated with them should understand that I am just an ordinary human. Moreover, after a long journey and a tiring wedding, I only desired some rest; yet another ritual awaited me, along with a sea of people wanting to glimpse the newlywed. This is the flaw of our culture.

As I tried to locate anything in my new home, I realised I didn't even know where my bedroom was or if there was a bedroom at all. I was clueless.

What if we had to sleep in a single room? What if this house only had a kitchen, one bedroom, and a bathroom? While pondering these thoughts, my phone rang—"Maasi."

I wanted to talk to her, but my mother-in-law insisted on speaking with her.

ᕱᕱᕱ

Next day

I sat amidst the piles of boxes, my mind filled with a whirlwind of thoughts and emotions. I couldn't shake the feeling of being overwhelmed by my new surroundings and responsibilities. The weight of societal expectations and the fear of disappointing my family loomed over me like a dark cloud.

"I need help understanding what to do," I whispered, my voice tinged with uncertainty. I am messy, but I can't afford to be. I need to keep everything in order." I glanced around the room, the disarray mirroring my mind's chaos.

Fatigue settled deep within my bones, making it challenging to find the energy to unpack. The exhaustion, both physical and emotional, seemed to consume me. Yet, I knew I had to push through to make this unfamiliar place my new home.

"I have to unpack," I reminded myself, my voice filled with determination. I longed for the comfort and familiarity of my previous life, but I also understood that change was inevitable. I took a deep breath, mustering the strength to begin the arduous task ahead.

In my heart, I hoped that my mother-in-law would lend a helping hand and that they would bond over this shared experience. But as the minutes turned into hours, I realised my expectations had been misplaced. The absence of my mother-in-law's assistance left her feeling disappointed and isolated.

As I continued unpacking, I couldn't help but reflect on my journey. "I am in a place where not even the air is familiar," I mused, my voice filled with melancholy. "Gone are the days of my books and video games. Now, I am no longer a carefree child but a wife."

The realisation hit me like a wave, washing over me with nostalgia and uncertainty. The new scents that filled the air and the food's flavours graced my plate—everything was foreign, starkly contrasting with the comfort of my family's home. It left me disconnected and unsure of my place in this new world.

The thought of eating brought a sense of apprehension. I didn't feel hungry or genuinely depressed, but I knew my lack of appetite would be perceived as a sign of distress. "They might think I'm upset or sick if I don't eat," I contemplated, my voice laced with concern.

At that moment, I realised the weight of the expectations placed upon me. I yearned for understanding, for someone to see beyond the surface and recognise the complexities of my emotions. The fear of being misunderstood and judged intensified, adding to my already heavy burden.

7

Love's Delicate Flame

01 September 2009

Our master's course was in full swing, and amidst our studies, three of our close friends, Ridhaan, Raj, and Akash, embarked on their entrepreneurial journey in the textile industry. It was an exciting time as they set up their small business.

On the day of their business opening, Raj approached me and inquired about Ridhaan. I couldn't help but smile at his curiosity. "How is Ridhaan doing?" Raj asked, his eyes filled with genuine concern.

"He's doing great," I replied confidently. "Ridhaan is someone I trust wholeheartedly. I don't surround myself with weak-minded friends."

Raj's response caught me off guard. He seemed taken aback by my words, and a flicker of disbelief crossed his face. "Kumudh, you're either crazy or pretending to be foolish," he retorted sharply before swiftly turning and walking away.

His abrupt departure startled me, and I struggled to comprehend his reaction. "Hey Raj, what the hell are you talking about?" I called out, a mix of frustration and confusion evident in my voice.

But Raj remained silent, offering no further explanation as he distanced himself. I couldn't help but feel annoyed at his dismissive attitude. It bothered me that he would say something so provocative without any clarity.

Lost in my thoughts, I mulled over his words, trying to make sense of them. I contemplated the meaning behind his statement, questioning if there was some hidden truth I had failed to recognise. However, after a while, I decided to let go of the topic, realising that dwelling on it would only lead to unnecessary frustration and confusion.

With a sigh, I returned home, leaving the incident behind me.

ᐳᐳᐳ

Since we returned from our memorable trip to Mandav, my friends have been insistent about Ridhaan's feelings for me. They claim he loves me, but I've never seen him in that light. Ridhaan has always been my best friend—a companion who understands me, supports me, and shares countless laughs with me. But beyond that, I have never felt any romantic inclination towards him.

While thinking about my ideal partner, I realised that I admire Shahid Kapoor and would want a husband with similar qualities. Several family members have told me I resemble Kareena Kapoor, which has fueled my imagination. It's like she is a reflection of me.

Since childhood, I firmly believed I would not settle for an arranged marriage. I strongly prefer a love marriage over an arranged one. The idea of meeting someone, falling in love organically, and choosing my life partner based on genuine feelings has always resonated with me. It's a path I yearn to walk upon, but thus far, I haven't encountered anyone who has sparked that special connection within my heart.

While my friends persistently advocate for Ridhaan's affection towards me, I remain firm. I can't force myself to feel something that isn't there. Love is a delicate emotion that cannot be conjured or manufactured at will. It is a flame that ignites naturally, spreading warmth and happiness.

Ridhaan, dear as he is to me, remains within the boundaries of friendship. And he understands and respects that. It's important to distinguish between the deep bond we share as friends and the romantic love that blossoms between two individuals. Sometimes, the most beautiful relationships are built on a foundation of friendship, where two souls find solace and support in each other without crossing that romantic threshold.

Sitting here, sharing my story with you, Ankit, I can't help but contemplate the intricacies of love and the complexities of human emotions. Sometimes, our hearts surprise us, revealing truths we never anticipated. The path to finding love is filled with uncertainty and unexpected twists. I couldn't predict my future, but I trusted that destiny would lead me to the right person who would ignite a spark within me.

So, I remained true to myself, acknowledging that my feelings, or lack thereof, for Ridhaan were genuine. Love could not be forced or manufactured, and honouring the sanctity of my emotions was vital. I believed that when the time was right, love would find its way to me, unfolding in a way that was meant to be.

ᐅᐅᐅ

24 November 2009

7:30 PM

I was in a flurry of excitement as I rushed to prepare for a wedding party. It was of one of my dear friends from our notorious "holy devil" group. I knew my gang would be there, ready to make unforgettable memories. As I hummed the tunes of "Lag Ja Gale Ke Phir Yeh," my phone suddenly rang, displaying the name of the real troublemaker... Guess who?

It was Ridhaan. "Hey, Ridhaan," I answered, curiosity piqued by his unexpected call.

"Kumudh, what colour are you wearing tonight?" Ridhaan's voice echoed with a hint of mystery.

"Dark cream," I replied, not thinking much of it. After all, it was just a simple question about my outfit."Well, Kumudh, let's meet at the party," Ridhaan suggested before abruptly ending the call.

Confusion settled within me as I tried to comprehend his request. "Hey, wait a minute. Why did he ask about the colour?"

ᏰᏰᏰ

8:30 PM

"Kumudh, let's go!" Riya's voice rang out, pulling me from my thoughts.

"Yes, Riya, I'm coming," I hastily gathered my things.

As I exited the house, I couldn't help but seek approval from my "Maasi." "How do I look, Maasi?"

"Kareena, my dear, you look stunning. Maybe tie one lemon and seven chillies in your hair for good luck," she playfully suggested.

"Come on, Maasi," I chuckled, knowing her superstitious penchant. "I'll be fine without them."

With a final farewell to my family, I set off for the party. Accompanied by Riya, we shared giggles and anticipation along the way.

"Hey, Riya, you look ravishing in that red dress," I complimented her, admiring her beauty.

"Oh, stop it, my Kareena. You look incredibly hot in this saree," she replied, returning the compliment with a mischievous grin.

We shared a lighthearted banter, finding solace in our deep friendship. The conversation flowed effortlessly as we exchanged stories, laughter, and the occasional secrets.

8

Boundaries of Strength

January 19, 2012

As I helped my mother-in-law arrange her clothes, Ajay's voice suddenly called out my name. "Kumudh," he said, his tone commanding my attention. I turned towards him, my heart racing with anticipation.

"Yes, Ajay," I responded, walking towards our room. I sensed something was on his mind, and my anxiety grew with each step.

"Come, relax here," Ajay motioned to the bed, shifting to create space for me. I sat down, feeling a mix of apprehension and curiosity.

At that moment, as Ajay's fingers touched my right shoulder, my heart skipped a beat. Memories of my past flooded my mind, memories of when I had asserted my boundaries with my ex-boyfriend. I had clarified that certain physical intimacy would wait until after marriage. But now, in the presence of Ajay, as his wife, I felt a sense of duty and obligation.

However, in an instant, I found my strength and stood up. I looked Ajay in the eyes and firmly told him to stop. His aggressive reaction took me aback, but I held my ground.

"What the fuck," Ajay shouted in frustration. Confusion and disappointment filled the room.

"Nothing, Ajay," I said, my voice steady despite my racing heart. "I just need to go to the washroom."

"Hmmm, come back quickly," Ajay responded, his tone tinged with annoyance.

I closed the door as I entered the washroom, creating a brief moment of solitude. The sound of running water filled the air as I approached the sink, my thoughts racing alongside the flowing tap.

In the peacefulness of the washroom, my mind started to wander, my thoughts becoming a chorus of conflicting emotions. I reflected on my choices and the path I had taken to reach this point.

As the water continued to run, I stared at my reflection in the mirror. My eyes held a mixture of determination and uncertainty. The moment seemed to freeze, allowing me to delve into the depths of my thoughts.

My mind was filled with emotions. I couldn't help but think about my ex and how different things were with him. But I quickly pushed those thoughts aside. This was my new reality, and I needed to face it head-on.

With a deep breath, I refocused my thoughts and resolved to confront the challenges before me. I knew that my journey with Ajay would be filled with ups and downs, and this was just the beginning.

Exiting the washroom, I approached Ajay, who still looked frustrated. "Done, or do you want anything else?" he asked, trying to maintain a sense of modesty.

"No, that's enough," I replied.

A sense of determination settled within me as I sat back down on the bed. Finding my voice and asserting my boundaries would be crucial in this relationship. I refused to let my past experiences define me or dictate my future.

With each passing moment, I was ready to face the challenges ahead. My journey with Ajay was beginning, and I was determined to find a way to make it work.

ᗧᗧᗧ

He then put his hand on my shoulder and started fumbling with the saree pin to open it, which I had put on my left shoulder.

After a bit of trouble, he finally opened it, and now he could see my breast materialise from my blouse.

He then started kissing perilously. As this is entirely new, I stabilise my lips.

I can see his desperation for sex while feeling his fast-moving lips on my lips.

While kissing, he touched my blouse and opened the button.

He squeezed me tight and started kissing my back while opening the bra's hooks.

He tries his level best to open the 'hooks,' but he fails,

Then I move ahead and unhook it. And there goes the first time in my life.

Bestowing my melons on a man who looks like my vagina.

He saw the shining white breast with a brownish nipple and immediately sat on his knees and started caressing and pressing it persistently with his hand.

I moaned Aaah as he pressed them gradually. He played 10 minutes with my nipple, and I was moaning with ecstasy.

His hands moved from my bum to my waist beneath my saree. Parted my saree above my stomach, kissed there, and licked my navel.

He then catches my hand and puts my hand on his dick above his jeans.

I was shocked. This happened in a moment, and I was like, what?

I didn't know what to do as this was my prime time.

Ajay's hands came down on my thighs. His hands were inside my thigh saree, slowly moving upwards. Till now, my saree pulled up to my bum. His hands were moving inside my pants on my bum. Then his hands were on my face.... Now he changed the position upside down. Now was above me. My legs were tied around his, and he was between my legs. My saree was almost to the waist. Now, Ajay broke the smooch. He attached my breast. He was craving my breast. I closed my eyes by now. My hands were in his hair, pressing him against my breast. I was moaning by now.

He then opened his jeans and started removing all my threads.

All my clothes were off in a flash, and I was not wearing anything. The prime moment I was showing my vagina to a guy. "I think my vagina was dripping beautifully"

And by scanning my womanhood, he started moving his hand on it and asked me to blow his dick.

I gave him a blowjob while moaning as he inserted his fingers in my women's hood.

*****

Now we are on the couch. The heavy, tall, and dark man is on me, a cute, beautiful and fair lady.

A moment where our bodies meet, there are no clothes in between.

There is a sense of heat and sensation which goes through my body.

He placed my hand on his tool and told me to stroke it again, and meanwhile, he was rubbing my womanhood.

By now, his penis was fully erect. I started sucking his penis. He had pre cum on his shaft; I was licking it. Now the lust for his penis was unbearable.

And I lose control, making a loud noise of 'Aaah.'

*****

What happened next, Kumudh, I (Ankit) said while burying my dick, as it is now in its last state to lose.

Why are you behaving like this, Ankit? Any bother articulated 'Kumudh.

No, Actually, yes. I want to go to the restroom. I spoke with a bit of shame.

OK, OK, no problem, go ahead. Kumudh responded.

I stood up from the recliner and hid my tool in the restroom.

*****

OK. Now I am all right, you continue, Kumudh.

From then on, he crawled to my holy place and raised one leg to grab most of it, to see and taste its saltiness and the love juices leaking from my divine part.

I am in a position where I can have a stunning view.

My one leg is in the air, and the licking wet vagina invites him to drink.

Now, in no time, he is between my legs, eating my woman's hood; I think he will eat everything he gets there.

He then inserts fingers in my womanhood... I mooned and cried. He ignored my tears and increased the number of fingers.

Indeed, let's switch gears and talk about something else; we will continue it tomorrow.

Tell me what happened when you attended your friend's marriage reception?

9
Unspoken Tensions and the Road Ahead"

24 November 2009

We arrived at "The Vitthalla" for the wedding function, and as Riya and I stepped into the vibrant party plot, I couldn't help but feel a surge of offence. Ridhaan was wearing the same colour as me—dark cream. My heart sank, and frustration bubbled within me. How could he do this? Didn't he realise my entire family was here, and this matching attire would only invite unnecessary attention?

A sense of betrayal washed over me as I recalled Ridhaan's phone call, where he casually inquired about my dress's shade. It all made sense now. He had intentionally chosen the same colour, knowing it would cause a stir. I met his gaze angrily, my eyes piercing through his very being. He understood my silent reproach, and the tension between us grew palpable.

Yet, I chose to keep my emotions in check. I couldn't afford to let my frustration spill over and give the others a reason to speculate about our relationship, which doesn't exist. I maintained a distance from Ridhaan, both physically and emotionally, aware that any display of our connection would only ignite unnecessary gossip.

Throughout the event, I kept my gaze fixed on the crowd, occasionally stealing glances in Ridhaan's direction. I noticed the flicker of remorse in his eyes, and for a moment, I wondered if I had misjudged his intentions. But the anger within me persisted, overshadowing any possibility of reconciliation.

As the party ended, Ridhaan approached me, his expression laced with guilt. He apologised for the matching concept, acknowledging the discomfort it had caused me. I listened to his words; my heart was torn between resentment and the desire to mend the rift that had formed between us.

At that moment, I realised that our friendship, which had once been a source of comfort and joy, had strained. The fear of disappointing each other and the unspoken tension between us had taken its toll. I longed for things to return to how they were before, but I knew it would require open and honest communication.

As Ridhaan offered to accompany me home, I hesitated for a moment. The late hour and the weight of our unresolved issues lingered in the air. But then, I realised that it was only through facing our problems head-on that we could return to the deep connection we once shared.

With a mixture of apprehension and hope, I accepted Ridhaan's offer, knowing that the journey ahead would require courage and vulnerability. It was time for us to address the underlying issues and have a deep conversation to pave the way for healing and understanding.

As we drove silently, unspoken words hung heavy in the air. I braced myself for the difficult conversation that awaited us, hoping it would strengthen our bond rather than break it further. The road ahead was uncertain, but I was determined to navigate it gracefully and honestly, hoping to restore the friendship we once cherished.

ΡΡΡ

Good morning, Kumudh," I greeted her with a warm smile.

"Good morning, Ankit," she responded, returning the smile.

"Shall we continue the scene we left in the middle yesterday?" I asked, my excitement evident in my voice.

Kumudh chuckled softly and replied, "Which one? We've had quite a few scenes."

I grinned, feeling a sense of connection with her as we delved into the world of her story. "The one on 19th January 2012, Kumudh," I clarified.

She paused for a moment, gathering her thoughts, before nodding her head in agreement. "Oh, alright," she said. "Let's pick up from there."

She took a deep breath, her eyes reflecting a mix of emotions, and began to narrate the scene we had left behind:

10

Bound by Love, Guided by Resilience

Ajay was playing with my woman's hood, and I am, too, enjoying copulation while forgetting all things.

He left me and stood; I understood it was the main course's turn.

He came on top of me, then spread my legs to access his tool near my tool.

Then he rubbed his tool on my woman's hood, injecting his device into mine, but he couldn't as it was very snug. After a few pushes, it went in, and I almost made a loud noise.

Blood on his tool...

I am breathing in rhythm,

*****

I was on a cloud, experiencing each bit of the session without remembering my hell past. Earlier, I never thought this would happen with Ajay.

But I endure this, as this is my destination.

*****

0. I'm sorry, Kumudh. I want to go to the washroom. I stopped her and ran towards the toilet.

Even now, I am masturbating, thinking of the scenes.

ᑭᑭᑭ

After 3 months
April 2 2012

After three long months of being away from my family, the day I eagerly awaited finally arrived. It was April 2, 2012, and my heart was filled with anticipation and joy. Today, my maternal uncle, "Maasi," and my dear cousins are coming to Bhiwandi, Maharashtra, to take me back with them.

This was a unique scenario where a bride spends only a few days with her husband's family and returns to her own home for some days. My circumstances were different, and the past three months had felt like an eternity without my loved ones by my side. But now, as I prepared for their arrival, a renewed sense of excitement and happiness filled the air.

As the clock struck three, I heard the familiar sounds of laughter and chatter outside. My heart skipped a beat, knowing that my family had finally arrived. With a smile, I hurriedly approached them, eager to embrace every one of them.

As I met my family members, their warm hugs and heartfelt greetings enveloped me in a sense of belonging. It was a beautiful reunion, and the joy in their eyes mirrored my own. After exchanging pleasantries and catching up on the latest news, we all sat down for a delicious lunch, savouring the flavours that brought us together.

As the meal ended, a sense of excitement filled the air. We were about to embark on a journey together, leaving my in-laws' house behind and heading to Mhow for some days, where we would spend the coming days. It was a chance to reconnect with my roots and bask in my family's love and warmth again.

We gathered our belongings and bid farewell to my in-laws, expressing gratitude for their hospitality. With every step we took towards the awaiting vehicle, my heart felt lighter, knowing I was surrounded by the people who loved and cared for me unconditionally.

As we set off towards Mhow, the conversations flowed effortlessly, bridging the gap of those three long months of separation. We shared stories, laughter, and even a few tears as we reminisced and looked forward to the future. In those moments of deep conversation, I realised the value of family—their unwavering support, ability to uplift and inspire, and unconditional love.

Amid those heartfelt exchanges, I couldn't help but feel a renewed sense of purpose. I knew I had a robust support system, no matter the challenges ahead. Together, we would navigate the intricacies of life, cherishing every moment and building beautiful memories.

As we arrived in Mhow, a sense of comfort washed over me. This was where I belonged, surrounded by my childhood's familiar sights and sounds. The days to come would be filled with love, laughter, and the rekindling of bonds that time had temporarily separated.

As the sun set on that eventful day, I couldn't help but feel an overwhelming sense of gratitude—gratitude to my family for their presence in my life and for the journey we were about to embark on together. This chapter of my life promised growth, love, and deep connections that would shape my story forever.

ᐯᐯᐯ

5 May 2012

Today was Saturday, a day that held mixed emotions for me. It marked the arrival of my husband, Ajay, who worked as an accountant and could only be with me on weekends. As I prepared for his arrival, a wave of conflicting thoughts washed over me.

I glanced at the calendar, realising a month had passed since I arrived in Mhow. At that time, my family and friends had bombarded me with questions about my life. They all sought reassurance that I was happy and content. And while I yearned to be truthful, I couldn't reveal the inner turmoil she experienced.

My mind drifted back to the memories of my previous life—a life of comfort and abundance that I had left behind. I knew I wasn't at ease with my current situation. The tiny house I now call home couldn't compare to the grandeur I once knew. But I buried these thoughts, determined to put on a brave face for the sake of my loved ones.

"I am happy here," I repeated as if trying to convince myself as much as the others. I had grown skilled at hiding my genuine emotions, shielding them behind a façade of contentment. My unspoken fears and desires weighed heavily, but I was determined to find my place in this new life.

The day arrived when my mother-in-law and Ajay travelled to Mhow to take me to their home.

As we stood at the railway station, waiting for our train, my heart raced with anticipation and anxiety.3

The atmosphere around us buzzed with the energy of travellers rushing to catch their trains while announcements echoed through the air.

"Oh God, here I go again, back to the unknown," I whispered to myself, my voice filled with apprehension. I reminded myself that this was life.

With hope, resilience, and a touch of timidity, I boarded the train, leaving behind the comfort of the familiar and venturing into the unknown realm.

As the train approached the platform, the rumbling of its engines grew louder. The sound reverberated through the station, heightening the sense of anticipation. I took a deep breath, steadying my nerves.

Little did I know that this journey would test my strength, resilience, and capacity for growth. But at that moment, as the train raced forward, I held on to the belief that I dared to live no matter what lay ahead.

11

Echoes of Destiny "

31 December 2009

My family surrounded me, bustling around the kitchen as we prepared dinner for the night's small gathering. The air was filled with anticipation as we welcomed the New Year together.

As the evening approached, the house came alive with the arrival of cars parked haphazardly in the yard. The chaos and commotion resembled a carnival, and it felt like I was trapped in a sideshow. My family began to make their way towards the terrace, and I reluctantly followed suit.

Meeting relatives was always the most dreaded part of these gatherings. The questions would start pouring in, prying into my life and aspirations. "What is Kumudh doing?" they would ask, seeking to gauge my every move. "She's just following Kareena," my Maasi would reply, attempting to brush off their inquiries. But deep down, I didn't care about their judgments. My cousins attended these events to avoid arguments with the family, and I, in turn, became the perfect one—the dutiful daughter playing her part.

As my parents faded into the crowd, I sought refuge in the spare room where my cousins had gathered. We went through the motions of discussing trivialities, recounting the mundane details of our past week. New mobile phones, holiday returns—it all felt inconsequential, and I yearned to escape the room and its mindless chatter. The sight of the monopoly board being set up only fueled my desire to flee.

Dinner seemed to drag on forever, and the anticipation of the upcoming new year weighed heavily on my mind. I sought refuge in the far corner of the terrace, away from the prying eyes of relatives and the incessant chatter of family members. Seated between my cousins, I tried to occupy myself by nibbling on a slice of cake. However, I couldn't continue after just half a bite. It was nothing short of disgusting.

Everyone else had finished their meals and resumed their conversations while my cousins and brother returned to their game of Monopoly. My brother, sitting beside me, glanced at the clock. It was 11:50, and the new year was ten minutes away. The atmosphere crackled with anticipation, a mix of excitement and anxiety.

And then, amidst the final moments of the countdown, my phone rang. The screen flashed the name Ridhaan. Caught up in the countdown frenzy, I momentarily ignored the call, assuming it was a simple New Year's wish. Little did I know that this call would shatter the illusion of a joyous evening.

Just as I was about to answer the call, my brother nudged me, pointing out the obvious. "Kumudh, your phone is ringing," he said, breaking through my reverie. I picked up the phone, my mind racing with possibilities, unaware of the unexpected turn this call would bring to the night.

Startled, I hastily answered the call, unaware that this conversation would set in motion a series of events that would challenge my expectations and redefine my path.

61

12
Destiny: The Radiant Red and the Airtel Register

Present-day 2019

Mr Writer, please tell me how you got my number and what interests you more about writing my memoir? Said Kumudh'

I leaned forward, my gaze fixed on Kumudh as she recounted the intriguing series of events that had brought us together. The twists and turns of fate enthralled me, and a mix of curiosity and admiration danced in my eyes.

"Kumudh," I began, my voice filled with sincerity, "the way I came across your number is a tale of chance encounters and unexpected connections. As you know, life has a way of weaving intricate threads, bringing people together in the most unexpected ways."

Kumudh leaned in closer, her curiosity piqued. "Please, tell me more," she urged, her voice filled with anticipation.

I smiled; my words had been carefully chosen to convey the magic of our meeting. "It was a day like any other, bustling with the ebb and flow of life. A figure caught my attention as I pursued my pursuits—a familiar face amidst the crowd. It was you, Kumudh."

Kumudh's eyes widened, a mix of surprise and intrigue washing over her. "You noticed me?" she asked, her voice carrying a hint of disbelief.

I nodded, my smile widening. "Yes, I did. Something was captivating about you, an air of mystery and resilience that stirred something within me. But it wasn't until later, through a mutual friend, that I began to unravel the layers of your story."

Kumudh's expression shifted, her curiosity growing. "What did this friend tell you?"

My voice lowered, my words carrying a tinge of intrigue. "He approached me and shared what he had heard—a whispered tale that left me curious and empathetic. He mentioned that you were taken, and even though you had a child, something about you captivated my attention."

Then he stretched and revealed that your husband left you because you also had an affair after your marriage. When my friend told me this, I felt he was telling me the truth...

But I didn't mind that, and later also used to following you.

Then once I got one more story about you,

That your husband left you because you are Mad.

Kumudh nodded, her eyes sparkling with a mix of vulnerability and strength. Life has had its share of challenges for me, but I refuse to be defined by them."

My admiration for Kumudh deepened as I spoke, my words laced with empathy. "That resilience, Kumudh, that unwavering spirit amidst adversity, fascinates me the most. The indomitable nature of the human spirit compels me to explore your memoir and share your story with the world."

A blush coloured Kumudh's cheeks as she averted her gaze, humbled by my words.

"Thank you, Mr. Writer. But there's more to this tale." Kumudh added.

I leaned forward, my curiosity intensifying. "Please, go on. I'm here to listen."

A mischievous glimmer danced in Kumudh's eyes as she continued, her voice filled with playful humour. "Well, another rumour reached my ears, Mr Writer. They said your husband left you because you weren't sensuous enough."

I chuckled, a mix of surprise and amusement playing on my lips. "Ah, the power of rumours. They can take on a life of their own, can't they?"

Kumudh grinned, her playful nature shining through.

"Indeed! But this time, I didn't trust it. Have you looked at yourself? You're like Kareena Kapoor—tongue-tied, so undeniably sexy!"

Laughter filled the air as I joined in, and the unexpected turn of the conversation strengthened our bond even further.

"Now, after hearing these stories, I knew I had to meet you," Kumudh. "But the predicament was that we were strangers. So, I set up a plan to connect with you digitally to find your contact number. I got an idea.

Kumudh leaned in closer, her curiosity piqued. "What's that?" she urged, her voice filled with anticipation.

ᐅᐅᐅ

As I followed your every move, I couldn't help but notice your radiant presence as you were entering the Mobile recharging shop. Clad in a fiery red top and fitted denim jeans, you instantly exuded an irresistible allure that caught my attention.

You were an embodiment of elegance and style in fashion. Your attire on that particular day showcased your innate ability to combine traditional elements with a modern twist effortlessly.

Your denim jeans hugged your curves perfectly, accentuating your slender figure and giving you a chic look. The fabric embraced your legs gently, revealing just enough to leave a lasting impression. The denim swayed rhythmically as you walked, adding a touch of allure to your every step.

Complementing denim jeans, the vibrant red kurta adorned your upper body. The colour came alive against your radiant complexion, illuminating your features and captivating all who saw you. The kurta's intricate designs and delicate embroidery spoke volumes about your appreciation for fine craftsmanship and attention to detail.

But the bindi, delicately placed between your eyebrows, added a touch of traditional charm to your ensemble. The small decorative mark, often associated with beauty and grace, was a focal point, drawing attention to your captivating eyes and framing your face with mystique.

As you walked through the streets, your attire became a tapestry of modernity and cultural heritage, blending seamlessly to create a mesmerising sight. Your confidence radiated from within, enhancing the appeal of your outfit and making you undeniably hot in every sense of the word.

"What's hot? I'm right here, Kumudh!" Startled.

As soon as you left the Mobile recharging shop, "I entered the recharge shop," I began,

"The shopkeeper asked me to write down the number. The place was filled with registers for networks like Airtel, Videocon, and others. There were approximately six registers in total."

With each moment, my attention was on stealing glances at your captivating figure. I needed to notice the colour of the register in which you entered your number.

However, a sudden realisation struck me, and I couldn't let the opportunity slip away. A mischievous grin spread across my face as I devised a plan. "After pondering for a while," I continued, "I decided to spend 300 rupees and wrote down the same number on each register for a recharge of 50 rupees each."

"I checked each register, one by one, eager to uncover a connection and wrote all six last numbers from all the registers. And there it was! Among the multitude of numbers, yours graced the Airtel register."

My eyes widened in surprise, a hint of a blush painting on my cheeks as the puzzle pieces fell into place. The story had reached its climax, and I couldn't help but share the conclusion with you. "Now you know the rest, Kumudh," I said, a mixture of anticipation and wonder.

13
Tangled Emotions

31 December 2009

I picked up the phone, and as soon as I answered, Ridhaan's voice poured through the receiver, tinged with a hint of intoxication. "You are like medicine to me," he began, his words carrying a weight that was hard to ignore. "When I see you smiling, it's as if all my pains melt away. When I think of you, I find a profound understanding of the meaning of life. Everything around me looks beautiful when you are by my side. You make me happy, Kumudh. You are the reason for my happiness. And I adore your long, flowing hair. I love everything about you, dear. You are my first and last love, Kumudh. I love you."

I listened intently to Ridhaan's impassioned declaration, although his inebriated state made it difficult to discern the depth of his emotions. Sensing my hesitation, I responded, "Okay, Ridhaan, we need to talk about this when you're sober." I cut the call, hoping to postpone the discussion until a more opportune.

But Ridhaan's voice grew louder, filled with desperation. "No, I want an answer now," he insisted, his words almost bordering on pleading.

Stunned by his insistence, I realised I hadn't reciprocated Ridhaan's feelings. Although my friends had warned me about his affection for me, I had dismissed it as a passing fancy. I struggled to find the right words when confronted with his raw vulnerability. "Ridhaan, my brother is here with me," I stammered, seeking refuge in the presence of my sibling.

But Ridhaan interrupted, his voice fraught with urgency. "No, Kumudh, I need an answer right now. I can't bear this uncertainty any longer."

Frustration mingled with my confusion as I raised my voice to convey my turmoil. "I said we'll discuss this tomorrow!" I shouted, the sharp click of the phone signalling the abrupt end of our conversation.

As I placed the phone down, a whirlwind of emotions enveloped me. The weight of Ridhaan's unrequited love hung heavy in the air, leaving me questioning my feelings.

14

The Veil: Tainted Vegetables and Confined Desires"

May 6, 2012

As we arrived at Bhiwandi, my mother-in-law and I decided to purchase vegetables at the market. Ajay, on the other hand, headed back home. Little did I know that this seemingly routine trip would turn into an eye-opening experience.

As we strolled through the bustling market, I couldn't help but notice my mother-in-law selecting vegetables that appeared to be past their prime. I was astonished. How could she choose such inferior produce?

My confusion led me back to a memory of peeling a potato and discovering that more than half of it was unusable. I had questioned my mother-in-law then, and she had blamed it on a dishonest vegetable seller, claiming that they had cheated her.

She had developed a habit of acquiring vegetables that the seller otherwise discarded. Curiosity got the better of me, and I confronted her about it.

"You know, I've noticed that the vegetables you're buying seem in poor condition," I ventured, hoping for an explanation.

My mother-in-law looked at me sharply, her eyes flashing with annoyance. "You don't need to interfere in my matters," she retorted. "I am the one who cooks the food, and I know what to buy."

I couldn't let it go. Concerned for our health, I said, "But these vegetables are rotten. They can't be good for us."

She paused momentarily; she looked at me sharply as if telling me to keep quiet.

15 June 2012

Frustration and confusion brewed within me as I struggled to comprehend my in-laws' strange behaviour. Ever since I arrived here from Mhow, they seemed like beings from another planet, acting in ways I couldn't fathom.

In the past, I used to be able to take charge of preparing my meals, but now, she doesn't allow me to set foot inside the kitchen. It's as if I've lost the privilege I once had.

To make matters worse, my mother-in-law has started delaying meals, leaving me hungry and dissatisfied. She also restricts me from preparing food for myself. Instead, she serves me leftover chapatis from previous meals, neglecting my needs and desires.

She only buys vegetables available at lower prices, regardless of their quality. I consume subpar produce, lacking the freshness and nutrition I am accustomed to. Occasionally, when she finds some fresh vegetables for herself and my father-in-law, I am left with only old chapatis accompanied by pickles.

And on those unfortunate occasions when even the pickles are absent, I am left with nothing more than a plain chapati. The mere thought of it sends shivers down my spine. Can you imagine the plight of a girl from a wealthy family, forced to consume such meagre provisions? I never would have imagined myself in such a situation, but here I am, with no alternative but to endure this life.

I long to confide in my "Maasi" and pour out all my grievances, but alas, I have proclaimed my contentment to them. I have concealed my genuine emotions, all in the name of preserving my family's honour and reputation.

Yet, with every passing day, the weight of this torment grows heavier, threatening to crush my spirit. How much longer can I endure this living nightmare?

15

Crossroads of Confessions

♡

1 January 2010

When I arrived at Riya's house, she wished me a happy New Year warmly. However, I couldn't reciprocate the sentiment, knowing that what I was about to reveal would shatter her joy. Taking a deep breath, I mustered the courage to speak.

"Riya, I need to tell you something," I began hesitantly.

She looked at me, her eyes filled with curiosity. "Yes, Kumudh," she replied, sensing the seriousness in my voice.

"Riya, someone proposed to me last night," I whispered, my words barely audible.

Her excitement was palpable as she bombarded me with questions, unable to contain her curiosity. "Oh my god, who's that guy? How does he look? Where is he from? How did he propose? And most importantly, what was your response?" Riya's voice rang with anticipation.

Taking a moment to compose myself, I answered softly, "Ridhaan proposed to me, Riya."

The room fell into stunned silence as Riya absorbed the news. "What...?" she finally managed to utter, her surprise evident.

"Yes, Ridhaan proposed to me," I reiterated, the weight of the situation sinking in.

Riya's initial shock transformed into frustration as she exclaimed, her voice filled with disappointment, "What? I told you before that he likes you, but you didn't believe me!"

I reached out to her, pleading for understanding amidst her growing anger. "Riya, please, I know you warned me, but you must believe me when I answer no. I don't have any feelings for Ridhaan."

Riya's eyes narrowed with anger as she confronted me about her feelings for Ridhaan. The hurt and frustration were palpable in her voice as she unleashed her pent-up emotions.

"You know what, Kumudh? I can't believe you're so blind to see it! I have feelings for Ridhaan!" she burst out, her words laced with frustration.

I took a step back, stunned by the intensity of her confession. The weight of her emotions settled heavily upon me as I struggled to find the right words to respond.

"Riya, I... I had no idea," I stammered, trying to comprehend the situation.

Riya's voice trembled with anger and sadness as she continued, "I've liked him for so long, and I thought you were my friend. I trusted you, Kumudh. How could you not notice? How could you not understand?"

Guilt washed over me as I realised the depth of Riya's feelings and my obliviousness. "Riya, I'm sorry. I never meant to hurt you, and I haven't hurt you. I had a clue about your emotions for Ridhaan," I admitted, my voice filled with remorse.

She let out a frustrated sigh, her eyes brimming with tears. "It's just... I thought you would be there for me, that you would understand. But now, it feels like everything has changed."

I approached her cautiously, my heart heavy with regret. "Riya, please believe me when I value our friendship above all else. I care about you. I want to make things right for you and Ridhaan."

Her anger softened slightly as she listened to my sincere words. "It's hard for me to trust you right now, Kumudh. This hurts more than you can imagine," she whispered, her voice tinged with vulnerability.

"I know I can't erase the pain that Ridhaan caused, but I promise to be there for you. I will support you if you want to pursue a relationship with Ridhaan. Your happiness matters to me," I assured her, my voice filled with genuine remorse.

Riya looked into my eyes, searching for sincerity. After a moment of contemplation, she nodded slowly.

Gently wiping away her tears, I reassured her, "Riya, please don't cry. I understand how much you care for me, but I can't force myself to feel something that isn't there. I promise to talk to Ridhaan and tell him you have feelings for him."

Riya's sobs gradually subsided as she looked at me with gratitude and sadness. "Thank you, Kumudh. It means a lot to me that you understand. Just... please be gentle with him. He's a good guy."

Nodding in agreement, I held Riya's hand, offering her solace. "I promise, Riya. I'll handle it delicately. Our friendship is too precious to let something like this come between us."

With a bittersweet understanding, we embraced, knowing that our bond would endure despite the turbulence. Together, we would navigate the complexities of love and friendship, supporting each other through every twist and turn.

After an hour...

"Riya, I will tell him about you... We'll find a way to handle this, okay?" I reassured her, taking hold of her trembling hands.

Tears streamed down Riya's face as she pleaded with me not to disclose her identity. "No, Kumudh, please... Ridhaan is a good guy. He likes you, and perhaps you're lucky that he does. If you want to do something for me, please say yes to Ridhaan," she sobbed.

I felt conflicted, knowing that I had no romantic feelings for Ridhaan. "Riya, I don't have any feelings for Ridhaan. We're just friends," I confessed, trying to make her understand. "I don't like him in that way, Riya."

Her desperation grew, and she clutched my arm, pleading desperately. "No, please, Kumudh. Don't tell him about me, okay? Please!"

"Listen, why don't you call him? Please let him know that your response is yes. Riya suggested. A glimmer of hope flickered in Riya's eyes.

No, not now, and I won't. I added.

ᕱᕱᕱ

Evening, at my place.

The room was dimly lit, casting a soft glow that reflected my conflicted emotions. I found myself sitting on the edge of the bed, clutching my phone tightly as if it held the answers to all my doubts and fears. It was 8:17 PM, a time etched into my memory forever.

Just as the haunting melody of "Lag Ja Gale" played softly in the background, piercing through the silence, my phone erupted into a frenzy of vibrations and flashes. The name on the screen sent a shiver down my spine—Ridhaan. With a deep breath, I mustered the courage to answer the call.

"Hello?" I said, my voice filled with a mixture of anticipation and trepidation.

And then, without warning, his voice cracked. Ridhaan's sobs echoed through the phone, reaching the depths of my soul. It was a sound I had never heard before, a raw vulnerability that tugged at my heartstrings. I could feel his pain, and it hurt me to my core.

"Kumudh, I have loved you since the day I joined your girls' group in college," he confessed, his voice trembling with emotion. "I joined the group because of you and fell in love with you, Kumudh."

His words hung heavy in the air, the weight of his feelings threatening to engulf me. At that moment, I couldn't help but feel an overwhelming sense of guilt and sympathy. How could I not? Ridhaan, my best friend, poured his heart out to me.

The conflict within me intensified as I grappled with my own emotions. I had dreamt of a love marriage my entire life, but not with Ridhaan. I cherished our friendship, but there was a void where romantic feelings should have been. I didn't want to deceive or lead him on, but I didn't want to see him suffer.

With a heavy sigh, I mustered the courage to speak my truth. "Ridhaan, I appreciate your honesty and value our friendship immensely," I began, my voice filled with compassion. "But I have to be honest with you, too. I don't have any romantic feelings for you."

My words hung in the air, the silence between us stretching into eternity. I could almost feel Ridhaan's heartbreak, and it tore at my own.

"But," I continued, my voice filled with determination, "I care about you deeply, Ridhaan. I don't want to see you unhappy. That's why I've decided to give us a chance. I say 'yes' to exploring a relationship, but I need time. Time to figure out my feelings and understand if there's a possibility for something more between us."

There was a pause on the other end of the line, and I held my breath, waiting for Ridhaan's response.

"Okay, Kumudh," he finally replied, his voice a mixture of relief and uncertainty. "You take your time. I understand."

The weight of his understanding hit me, and tears welled up in my eyes. At that moment, I realised the actual depth of our bond. Ridhaan's love for me had brought us to this crossroads, and now it was up to me to navigate the uncertain path ahead.

As the conversation ended, I whispered a silent prayer, hoping that time would bring clarity for Ridhaan and me. Little did I know that this decision would set events that would forever change our lives.

16

A Doll's Imprisonment: Marital Rape and Desperate Yearnings

5 June 2012

As the days wore on, I was suffocating in this stifling environment. Every inch of the house was off-limits to me. My mother-in-law had imposed strict rules, forbidding me from touching the refrigerator, the television, or the air conditioner. It was like living in a ghostly mansion, void of any life or activity.

One particular incident stands out vividly in my mind. I sat in the living room, engrossed in a television show that momentarily whisked me away from my suffocating reality. Just as I began feeling a glimmer of escape, my mother-in-law abruptly switched off the TV, leaving me in darkness. To my horror, she then locked the door, imprisoning me within the confines of my bedroom.

Days turned into weeks, and the only time the door to my room swung open was when my mother-in-law would begrudgingly bring me a meagre meal or on the rare occasion when Ajay, my husband, came to visit on weekends. It was as if my existence had been reduced to a hidden secret, concealed away from the world.

Occasionally, the door would crack open when our next-door neighbours or relatives paid a visit. In those fleeting moments, they would glimpse me as if on display while my captors paraded me as a contented and happy household member. Despite the limited interaction, I cherished those brief conversations with the outside world, a taste of the life I once knew.

The neighbours were my lifeline, offering a glimmer of hope amidst the darkness that consumed me. They genuinely cared for me and extended their kindness, providing a sense of connection I desperately craved. Engaging in conversations with them brought solace to my heart, if only for a fleeting moment.

However, my respite was short-lived. Whenever I conversed with the neighbours, my father-in-law's cruel words would slice through the air like a bitter wind extinguishing my heart's warmth. He would hurl abusive remarks to demean and remind me of my place. And my mother-in-law, ever the enforcer of their twisted reality, would promptly ask the neighbours to leave our house, extinguishing the flicker of joy that had briefly illuminated my life.

In the face of such oppression, I found myself torn between the solace of connection with the outside world and the torment inflicted upon me by my own family. It was a battle that raged within me.

ppp

July 2012 (AFTER ONE MONTH)

My life feels like it's being consumed within the confines of this room. It's as if there's no future beyond these walls. I have nothing to do, spending entire days cooped up here. To make matters worse, there are times when the electricity board cuts off our connection due to unpaid bills, leaving us without power for months.

I can't help but feel like a mere doll in their eyes. I am imprisoned within these walls from Monday to Friday, and on weekends, I am fucked here.

It's become painfully clear that I am no longer his wife. I am merely an object, a sex toy, used for his pleasure alone. This phase of my life feels like an endless cycle of marital rape, where I have no say or control over my body.

In this suffocating phase, I feel trapped with no way out. The Indian courts' stance on marital rights is disheartening; a husband can claim ownership over his wife's body whenever his dick gets erect. No matter the time, even at 3 AM, he can disregard her boundaries, forcibly pulling up her saree without consequence.

This reality, devoid of choice and respect, has left me helpless and confined. It's a situation I never envisioned for myself, and I yearn for a future where I can break free from this suffocating existence.

17

Love – Whispers in the Enchanted Garden

3 January 2010

As the New Year's celebration ended, our college reopened after two days. I mustered up the courage to tell Ridhaan about Riya, uncertain how he would react. I sat him down and revealed the truth, hoping he would understand and maybe even let me go.

But instead of the reaction I expected, Ridhaan exploded. His face turned red, and he shouted at me, "No! You can't say that, Kumudh. Please, don't say it, okay?"

Taken aback by his outburst, I realised he must have had some idea that Riya had feelings for him. However, she had never expressed them directly to him, which left him in a state of uncertainty. he added

Ridhaan's response shocked me. He pleaded with me, urging me to forget Riya and focus on him.

*****

With nervous anticipation, Ridhaan mustered up the courage to invite me to the garden, hoping to spend quality time together.

I nodded, okay.

As we entered the peaceful sanctuary, the sounds of laughter and chatter from other students faded into the background, leaving an air of tranquillity behind.

My eyes widened as I took in the beauty of the surroundings. The vibrant hues of the flowers and the gentle rustling of leaves in the breeze created a mesmerising atmosphere.

Sensing my apprehension, Ridhaan took my hand and smiled reassuringly. "Don't worry, Kumudh. We can take all the time you need. Let's enjoy the peace and serenity of this garden together."

My blush deepened, but a glimmer of gratitude shone in my eyes. Ridhaan's understanding and patience comforted me. Slowly, we explored the garden hand in hand, our steps cautious and measured.

We found a secluded spot beneath a canopy of trees, where the golden sunlight filtered through the branches, casting dappled patterns on the ground. Ridhaan gently guided me to sit on a wooden bench, creating a safe space to open up at my own pace.

As we sat in companionable silence, Ridhaan shared anecdotes from his life, carefully choosing his words to make me feel at ease. He noticed me stealing glances at him, my eyes filled with curiosity and intrigue. With each passing moment, a delicate bond began to form between us.

My shyness gradually faded, replaced by a growing comfort in Ridhaan's presence. I mustered the courage to share snippets of my life, dreams, and aspirations. Ridhaan listened intently, eyes locked on me as if my every word held the key to his happiness.

Time seemed to stand still in that idyllic garden as our connection deepened. Our laughter mingled with the rustling leaves, creating a symphony of joy and affection.

ᑭᑭᑭ

From that day forward, Ridhaan and I became inseparable. He consciously tried to spend more time with me, cherishing every moment. Our rendezvous became a daily ritual, meeting at 3:30 PM in the enchanting garden of DAVV.

Ridhaan's affection for me became evident in the little gestures he made. He showered me with love and care, often doing silly things that made me laugh. I adored those goofy moments that brought joy to our relationship, but occasionally, his antics tested my patience and irritated me.

One day, I casually mentioned that I was planning to get a haircut, not thinking much of it. To my surprise, Ridhaan's reaction was far from supportive. He looked at me wide-eyed and exclaimed, "Kumudh, please don't do that. I love your long hair. It suits you so well."

His sudden outburst caught me off guard. I couldn't help but smile at his possessiveness and the genuine concern he expressed for something as trivial as my hair. It reminded me how deeply Ridhaan cared for me, wanting everything about me to remain as it was.

At that moment, I realised that love could be beautiful and unpredictable. Ridhaan's fierce protectiveness over me, even in matters as small as my hairstyle, was a testament to the depth of his feelings. It made me appreciate him even more and reinforced our bond as we continued to navigate the intricacies of our relationship.

ᑭᑭᑭ

March 1, 2010

We had been together for 2 months, and the feeling of falling in love was unlike anything else. Falling - it's the only accurate verb to describe it. It consumes your thoughts and heart, and nothing else seems to matter. Looking back on it now, that's exactly what it felt like, a free fall into an unknown abyss. And the surprising part is that it can happen when you least expect it, even with someone you've crossed paths with.

The feeling of falling in love with me was a whirlwind of emotions that swept me off my feet, leaving me exhilarated and filled with a newfound sense of joy. It was as if the world had suddenly burst into vibrant colours, and every moment spent with Ridhaan became a treasure to cherish.

His presence had an enchanting effect on me, captivating my heart and mind. I daydreamed about him, his smile becoming light in my thoughts.

With each passing interaction, my feelings grew more robust, like a delicate flower blossoming under the warm rays of the sun. His laughter was music to my ears, and his words held the power to uplift my spirits. I felt truly alive in his company, as if every moment was imbued with magic.

It was a pivotal moment in our journey together when I could no longer hide my emotions. The weight of my feelings pressed upon me, and I knew I had to let Ridhaan see the depth of my affection. Heart pounding, I mustered the courage to express what had been silently growing within me.

I vividly recall when I realised I was falling in love with Ridhaan. We were snuggled up in a cosy movie theatre, lost in the magic of the film. For some reason, without any warning, the words just tumbled out of my mouth, "I love you too," but in Russian. "Я ЛЮБЛЮ ТЕБЯ."

In that instant, I wanted to downplay the moment's significance, even test the waters of his reaction. To my surprise, though he didn't utter a single word, his eyes locked onto mine with a knowing glint.

Let me GOOGLE it," he confessed with a mischievous grin.

Part of me wondered if I had rushed into expressing those words too quickly, but deep down, I knew the feelings were genuine. As crazy as it seemed, it felt strangely natural. Lost in my thoughts, Ridhaan interrupted, his voice filled with curiosity.

"Are you busy for the next 80 years?" he asked, causing me to pause. Confused, I inquired, "Why?" His response was laced with a hint of playfulness: "I thought we could hang out or something."

At that moment, it became clear that Ridhaan loved me, and I loved him. Without hesitation, I replied with a resounding "Yes."

"Yes," I said, my voice filled with the certainty of my heart.

His eyes met mine, and I saw a flicker of recognition, a glimmer of emotions mirrored in their gaze. It was a moment of vulnerability, of baring our souls to each other, unsure of the future. And then, with a tender smile, His voice reached my ears.

"I feel the same way," we whispered, words carrying a sense of wonder and joy. In that instant, a surge of happiness washed over me as if I were floating on a cloud. Realising that our hearts beat in harmony filled me with a sense of belonging and contentment.

From that day forward, falling in love with him became a beautiful journey of discovery and growth. Every smile, every touch, every shared moment felt like a precious gift.

We embarked on deepening our connection, getting to know each other's quirks and intricacies, and building a bond based on trust, understanding, and mutual respect.

Falling in love with him was exhilarating yet comforting, like finding a missing piece of the puzzle that completed me. His presence ignited a fire within my soul, fueling my aspirations and encouraging me to become the best version of myself.

Our love grew more profound as we continued to traverse the twists and turns of life together. It challenged me to be vulnerable, to open my heart fully, and to embrace the beautiful uncertainty of our shared future. With him by my side, I knew we could conquer any obstacle together, for our love was a force that knew no bounds.

18

Finding Hope in Unexpected Places

November 2012

I sat alone in my small, dimly lit room, the walls adorned with faded posters and peeling paint. My only companions were the whirring fan overhead, the creaky bed that had become my refuge, and a few cherished belongings scattered around the space. Each day, the room transformed from a mere shelter into my world.

As the months went by, I engaged in a peculiar routine. From Monday to Friday, I pour my heart out to the inanimate objects surrounding me, and they watch me mooning on the bed on Saturday and Sunday. The fan became my confidante, spinning tirelessly above me, whispering secrets only the still air could hear.

Sitting cross-legged on my worn-out bed, I would recount my daily triumphs and tribulations, sharing my hopes and dreams. The bed listened attentively, absorbing every word, providing solace in its comforting embrace. It had become a silent witness to my journey, an unwavering pillar of support.

With its sparse decor, the room became a sanctuary where thoughts bloomed, and imagination ran wild. In the absence of human company, I discovered solace in the companionship of my trusted allies. They were my sounding board, reflection, and sounding board, always there to lend an ear, even if it was just the fan's hum or the gentle creaking of the bed.

But when the weekend arrived, my conversations shifted. The fan spun on, but I no longer directed my musings toward it. I spent my Saturdays and Sundays sprawled on the bed, with Ajay murmuring in pain as he stroked me. I only gazed out the window at the world beyond in despair. The objects in the room observed me empathetically, understanding the longing in my gaze.

I yearned for human connection, friends' lively banter, and shared laughter and warmth. The walls that had been her sanctuary suddenly felt confining, echoing her loneliness. The fan whirred above, trying its best to fill the void, but its attempts fell short on these desolate weekends.

My conversations became silent, replaced by a yearning for something more. I longed for the day when the joy of human interaction would supplement my companionship with the fan and the bed. Dreams of new friendships and unforgettable conversations danced in her mind, igniting a spark of hope.

As the days turned into weeks and the weeks into months, my room continued to be my haven, where I found solace and comfort. I cherished conversations with the fan and the bed, knowing they were my steadfast allies on this lonely journey.

ᎶᎶᎶ

10 November 2012

I remember that day vividly, for it was the day I discovered the depths of hunger. The date etched itself into my memory to remind me of my desperation. As the hours crept by and the sun descended, my in-laws neglected to offer me even a morsel of food. I sat patiently in the locked room, hoping my meal would arrive soon. It was 5 p.m., and the pangs in my stomach grew unbearable, and I realised I hadn't eaten anything since morning.

Driven to desperation by the gnawing hunger within me, I mustered all the strength I had left and the courage to knock on the door of my room. "Mummy Ji," I called out, my voice trembling with anxiety and longing.

I waited, my heart pounding, as the seconds turned into minutes. Finally, after what seemed like an eternity, my mother-in-law heard my plea and reluctantly approached me. Frustration and annoyance marked her face as she asked sharply, "What the fuck happened? Why are you screaming?"

Tears welled up in my eyes, a mixture of sorrow and the physical pain of hunger. "Mummy, I am hungry," I managed to say, my voice quivering. "Please, offer me something to eat."

She looked at me, her expression a mix of indifference and helplessness. "From where am I supposed to give you food?" she retorted, her words laced with resignation. "There is nothing to eat. Tomorrow, Ajay will bring money, and then I can buy food. But today, you must endure sleeping with an empty stomach."

Her words hit me like a dagger, and I could feel my strength waning. The reality of my situation sank in, and I realised that my plea had fallen on deaf ears. The pain of hunger seemed to amplify, consuming my entire being.

At that moment, I felt an overwhelming mix of emotions—frustration, anger, and a deep sense of helplessness. How had I reached this point where my most basic needs were neglected? Hunger gnawed at me, not only physically but emotionally as well. I had no choice but to confront the harsh reality that hunger had become my constant companion, and that night, it would claim victory over me again.

ᐅᐅᐅ

Next Day

The last time I ate a single bite of food was yesterday, and I've lost count of the glasses of water I've consumed. It's a challenging situation, and on top of it all, I don't even have enough money to buy something for myself. I need to find a way out of this predicament, and the solution that comes to mind is getting a job. If I can secure employment, it would mean freedom from this confining room, and most importantly, I'll be able to afford the food I've been longing for.

But how can I find a job in this situation? Ajay only visits for two days, and my in-laws would never allow me to work. It's a challenging dilemma that I need to resolve.

As I ponder the possibility of finding a job, I suddenly hear a familiar voice—Neha, my sister-in-law. Usually, her arrival brings me distress, but this time I feel a glimmer of hope. Perhaps she could help me find a job.

However, deep down, I doubt whether she'll lend a hand. She shares the same mindset as her parents, and their disapproval of me seeking employment might also be ingrained in her.

19

Veiled Flames: Love's Unraveling Thread

10 July 2010

(after six months of our relationship)

I had always been deeply connected to my culture and faith, so when I entered into a relationship six months ago, it sent me a wave of identity shock. Doubts plagued my mind: Was I doing the right thing? I knew I wasn't, but I stubbornly clung to denial.

I tried to use those fundamental aspects of my identity to justify my actions. I convinced myself that dating was typical and everyone else in the community did it. But the truth was, having a boyfriend was hypocritical, and no amount of rationalisation could change that. Still, I fulfilled my religious duties, attempting to find some balance.

As my connection with Ridhaan grew, a strange but exhilarating sensation overcame me. It was as if I had finally unlocked the door to teenage rebellion. I found myself defying my parents by concealing our relationship. Lying about my whereabouts became second nature, an art I had mastered without a second thought.

The thrill came from the fact that Ridhaan belonged to a lower caste. He hailed from a Hindu community but wasn't a Marwari like me. Yet, he understood the gravity of our situation and the need for secrecy. This understanding became the foundation of our relationship. It meant preceding regular dates, avoiding restaurants and the local mall, and fearing the prying eyes of family, friends, and relatives who could catch us together.

But despite the obstacles, we shared stolen moments of joy, hidden smiles, and the electricity that crackled between us whenever we managed to steal a few precious moments alone. Our love was shrouded in secrecy, a forbidden flame that burned brightly in the shadows.

As the days turned into months, the weight of our clandestine affair began to take its toll. The constant fear of being discovered, the limitations on our freedom, and the nagging guilt ate away at us. Yet, the allure of our rebellious romance held us captive, and we couldn't tear ourselves away from the exhilarating dance on the tightrope of our forbidden love.

Little did we know that the threads of our secret would soon start unravelling, threatening to expose the fragile web we had woven. But for now, we held on tightly to each other, seeking solace in the stolen moments and vowing to defy the norms that sought to keep us apart.

ϷϷϷ

12 July 2010

My eyes were heavy this morning, and a wave of nausea washed over me. I couldn't shake the feeling that something was amiss; something was about to go wrong.

After a seemingly good day at college with my boyfriend, I bounded home, my heart filled with happiness and an inexplicable excitement. Upon entering the house, I greeted my "Maasi" and Nani, eager to change and unwind.

But just as I settled into my room, my cousin barged in, announcing that Nani wanted to speak with me. It struck me as odd because I had just exchanged greetings with her, and she hadn't mentioned anything before. My heart skipped a beat, fearing that trouble was on the horizon. I swiftly reached for my phone, hastily deleting any questionable pictures, messages, and even social media accounts, attempting to prepare for the unknown.

Nervously, I made my way downstairs, entering the drawing room. To my surprise, my maternal uncle was waiting there with his dramatic and worried expression. My heart sank as a surge of anxiety coursed through me. It couldn't possibly be what I feared, could it?

My maternal uncle began speaking, and with each word, my heart raced faster, tears welling up in my eyes. "Are you involved with a boy? Do you have a boyfriend?" he interrogated, his tone laced with concern and disapproval.

Caught off guard, I mustered a feeble response, "Uh, no?"

That's when my "Maasi" presented pictures on her laptop. Shock and disbelief flooded my mind. "What the fuck?" I exclaimed internally. There, displayed before me, were images of Ridhaaan and me, hands intertwined, captured in intimate moments.

Speechless, tears streamed down my face. How did they acquire these pictures? All my social media accounts were private, and I never shared anything publicly. I needed answers and clarification on how these images reached their hands. Someone had betrayed my trust, sending my family screenshots from various platforms.

My family urged me to explain, to defend myself, but I couldn't find the words. Numbness enveloped my body and mind, rendering me incapable of coherent thought.

Then, my maternal uncle demanded my phone. I dashed upstairs to retrieve it in a panic, returning swiftly to his side. As he rummaged through my messages and pictures, my heart raced with trepidation. He found nothing incriminating, yet he refused to relinquish my phone, holding onto it tightly.

My mother, consumed by anger and disappointment, paced the room, her voice raised in disbelief. The air grew heavy with her words as she expressed her disdain and labelled my actions as repulsive and disgraceful. She couldn't fathom that her daughter could be involved with a boy.

If your family is anything like mine, you might think this situation is dramatic. And you would be right; it didn't have to be this way. But my family members were far from laid-back. They adhered strictly to tradition, and the thought of deviating from it felt like their world was collapsing.

I remained silent, quietly observing my family's reactions. Was this such a huge issue? No, it wasn't. I answered myself, realising how deeply entrenched traditional values were within my family and how intolerant they were regarding such matters.

Confusion etched across their faces, myriad emotions mirroring the whirlwind storm brewing within me. It was as if time stood still, their eyes locked onto mine, awaiting an explanation that would unravel the mystery shrouding my decision.

Amidst the chaos, my "Maasi" stood as a pillar of support. She encouraged me to open up and confide in her, desperately wanting to understand what was happening. I was too embarrassed to speak, and the thought of breaking up with Ridhaaan wasn't an option for me.

Hysterical sobs racked my body as the world blurred into a painful haze. I retreated to my room, weeping the rest of the day and night. The embarrassment of exposure, the weight of their judgment, and the uncertainty of their subsequent actions weighed heavily upon me.

<h1 style="text-align:center">20</h1>

<h1 style="text-align:center">The Gaze that Beckoned</h1>

December 2016

It was a chilly December day, and as I stepped off the train, a gentle breeze brushed against my skin, mingling with the scent of green trees on platform no.1. My "Maasi" had accompanied me to the station to bid me farewell before my journey to Mumbai. But contrary to what you might assume, I wasn't heading to my in-laws' house. No, I was off to spend my holiday at my cousin's residence instead.

Standing near the end of the platform, with only a few scattered souls around, the world seemed peaceful and quiet. Little did I know that this seemingly ordinary day held something extraordinary in store for me.

As the train finally arrived, Aarav and I respectfully touched "Maasai's" feet, expressing our gratitude for her presence. We then embarked on our journey, leaving her behind. Finding our seats, I settled in, feeling a sense of anticipation building within me.

And then, I saw him.

There he was, a vision that captured my attention and sent a shiver down my spine. A handsome young man with tousled brownish hair, donning a white medical coat, tan pants, and a sleek black backpack. His gaze wandered, searching for his seat, and fate had it that his assigned spot was right next to mine.

My heart skipped a beat as he placed his backpack in the overhead compartment and walked towards the door. It was as if time stood still, and I couldn't help but be captivated by his enigmatic aura. Was he lost in deep contemplation or lost in his world? I yearned to know his story and understand the thoughts racing through his mind. Where was he going? Where had he come from?

Without any logical explanation, my intense curiosity and fascination washed over me. An unexplainable magnetic pull drew me towards this stranger, urging me to unravel the mysteries hidden behind his captivating gaze.

21

Embracing Motherhood, Embracing Strength

1 February 2013

The past two months have been quite a journey at this construction company. The work can be incredibly tedious as a computer operator, but surprisingly, I am happy here.

(Author talk)

"So now you're free from that room?" I asked, curiosity brimming in my voice.

Kumudh, I let out a sigh, my smile fading slightly. "Not exactly. My mother-in-law still locks me up for half the day.

If I don't work this job, I fear she will keep me confined all day."

I frowned, sympathy evident in my eyes. "Oh, I see. But at least now you're earning. You can do something with the money," I suggested, trying to find a silver lining.

A bitter chuckle escaped Kumudh's lips. "Yes, that's what I thought too, when I received my first salary. But things changed in seconds."

I leaned in, and my curiosity piqued. "What happened?"

"My husband took my ATM card," Kumudh confessed, a hint of frustration seeping into her words. "I only receive 20 rupees daily from my mother-in-law for my transportation expenses. It's barely enough to cover my daily commute, and I'm left with nothing."

My eyes widened, disbelief etched on my face. "That's hardly anything! So, you're left with only 600 monthly rupees after travelling expenses?"

Kumudh nodded, her voice filled with resignation. "Yes, exactly. In one month, I earn five thousand four hundred rupees for my in-laws, but it feels like a drop in the ocean."

My brow furrowed as I tried to make sense of the situation. "Okay, but now that you're earning, your in-laws don't provide you with a better meal? You're contributing to their household, after all," I insisted, hoping for a glimmer of positivity.

A wistful smile appeared on Kumudh's face, tinged with sadness. "No, unfortunately. I still receive the same old food as before, and to make matters worse, I don't even get my tiffin sometimes."

My expression turned sombre as I understood the gravity of Kumudh's situation. "I'm really sorry to hear that. It must be tough for you."

Kumudh shook her head, grateful for my concern. "Thank you, Ankit, but I'm unsure if there's a way out then. I was trapped in that cycle, trying to please everyone while sacrificing my happiness."

ᛦᛦᛦ

10 April 2013

I managed to secure leave from my office for the first time to attend a family marriage with my in-laws. Little did I know that this auspicious day would also mark the end of my career.

My excitement grew as we gathered in the marriage house, preparing for the joyous occasion. The thought of indulging in the delectable feast awaiting us filled my mind. Just as I was lost in my reviews of the mouthwatering food, my mother-in-law entered the room, holding a tray adorned with the precious jewellery that my family had gifted me during my marriage.

"Today, I want you to wear these and display our family's wealth," she proudly said, handing me the intricately designed pieces.

Look at these." They want to showcase richness today," I forgot I was not in my room I said while seeing the fan.

Time passed, and I gracefully draped a saree when an unexpected sensation caught my attention. A dampness in my panties made me believe that my period, which had been delayed for the past two months, had finally arrived. Anxious to confirm, I discreetly checked, only to find it was merely a white discharge. Shaking off the concern, I refocused on getting ready, determined to enjoy the festivities.

An hour later, a wave of pain coursed through my abdomen, signalling the impending arrival of my period. However, the pain felt different from my usual monthly cramps, causing a sliver of worry to creep into my mind. I brushed aside the concerns, determined to enjoy the evening and the feast that awaited.

A distant voice called out my name as I savoured a bite of delicious food. At first, I dismissed it, engrossed in the flavours dancing on my palate. However, the urgency in

Ajay's voice caught my attention. Handing my plate to my sister-in-law, I hurried towards Ajay, curious about the speed in his tone.

As I approached him, he playfully raised his leg, causing a momentary shock to ripple through me. How could he expect me to remove his shoes in front of approximately 500 people? The thought raced through my mind, leaving me momentarily flustered.

I hesitated momentarily, but then I couldn't deny his request. I gracefully seated myself beside him, focusing on untying his shoelaces. However, his cousin, clearly uncomfortable with the situation, demanded that I stop this act. Ajay dismissed him, urging me to continue.

Feeling embarrassed and determined, I carried on with the task. As I reached the final stages of removing Ajay's shoes, fate intervened, and I stumbled, falling to the ground. The commotion drew the attention of those around us, including Abhishek, my husband's cousin, who rushed to my aid. However, Ajay, seemingly unfazed, remained motionless.

"Call the doctor !" Abhishek yelled urgently, concerned for my well-being.

*****

As the doctor arrived, it became apparent that my fall resulted from a sudden jump in blood pressure and a lack of glucose in my system. And now, I lie in the hospital's general ward, anxiously awaiting the reports that would shed light on my condition.

The doctor entered the room, breaking the suspense. "Congratulations," he announced, a smile forming on his face. "You're pregnant."

The room seemed to light up as those words sank in. The joy and happiness that flooded my heart were overwhelming. At that moment, a profound sense of honour washed over me.

Finally, I will have a companion on the horizon who will be there with me through life's trials and tribulations. The anticipation grew within me, and I longed for my baby's arrival, which would bring them a renewed sense of happiness and purpose.

The prospect of having a companion on the horizon filled me with an overwhelming sense of joy and purpose. As the reality of my pregnancy settled in, I couldn't help but feel a profound sense of gratitude. A tiny life was growing within me, a precious gift that would accompany me through life's trials and tribulations.

As I lay in the hospital bed, thoughts of the future intertwined with the present. The journey ahead might be filled with uncertainties, but knowing I would soon have a precious little one by me filled me with unwavering hope.

ᑭᑭᑭ

1 May 2013

I had made a tough decision to leave my job, believing my husband would care for me during this crucial time. Unfortunately, I was proven wrong. Every time I asked him for money for a checkup, he would dismiss it, claiming that our expenses were already overwhelming and his salary was not enough. That moment marked a turning point for me. I resolved never to depend on him for a single rupee again, and that's when I decided to start giving tuition in my room.

The scarcity of funds forced me to delay my checkup until the third month when it should have been done in the first. Despite the circumstances, I secured three students for tuition, earning a modest 1500 rupees. I had to spend 200 rupees on my checkup and another 50 on an auto fare. I stored the remaining amount in my ALMIRA for future use, although my mother-in-law had a habit of helping herself with it without asking.

It frustrated me whenever she took my hard-earned money, but I learned to keep my composure. I knew losing my temper wouldn't solve anything, so I quietly endured the situation. To maintain my inner strength and positivity, I repeated a series of mantras to myself:

"I am embarking on the journey of motherhood. God has blessed me with a companion who will always be there for me. I can be the best version of myself, no matter the circumstances. This path may be challenging, but I am confident I can overcome it."

These words became my refuge, reminding me that I had the strength and determination to face any obstacles that came my way.

22
Serendipitous Encounters on the Midnight Train

December 2016

As the train made a few stops, the crowd grew thicker, and more people began piling in. Among them, he appeared, taking the seat in front of mine. I felt an immediate urge to strike up a conversation, but being the type who hesitates to approach strangers, I didn't expect it to happen naturally. However, against my usual instincts, I mustered the courage and decided to come to him.

"Excuse me," I said, "Are you a doctor? And where are you headed?"

Surprisingly, this simple question sparked a few minutes of small talk. "Yes," he replied, "I'm going to Mumbai for a shift from a hospital in Indore."

"Oh, so you're from Indore?" I asked, genuinely interested.

"Yes, I'm going to Mumbai for a function," he explained. "My name is..."

But before he could finish, Aarav, my son, caught his attention. "Your son?" he pointed with a friendly smile.

"Yes," I responded, "His name is Aarav. He is usually shy around strangers, but I guess he's making an exception today."

We exchanged pleasantries, and then, unexpectedly, the conversation fell into silence. Time seemed to stretch, and I felt pressured to say something to keep the interaction going. Thoughts raced through my mind, urging me, "Say something, anything!" Yet, the words refused to escape my lips.

Unbeknownst to me, he was experiencing the same dilemma. At that moment, I mistakenly believed that I had lost his interest. Anxiety coursed through me, hindering my ability to find the right words.

As I desperately contemplated my next move, Aarav chimed in, breaking the silence. "Mumma, Buku," he said, signalling his hunger.

Relieved by the interruption, I took out the delicious dinner my "Maasi" had packed and enjoyed it. Eventually, it was time to retire to my middle berth for the night. I assumed the doctor had secured the central berth across from mine, but to my surprise, fate had a different plan.

The doctor had been assigned the lower berth in my row, while a woman passenger took the middle berth in the opposing row. Suddenly, the woman raised her voice, expressing her concern about the instability of her central berth due to her size. Without hesitation, the doctor offered a solution.

"I can sleep on the middle berth," he kindly suggested. "You can take my berth."

My mind immediately jumped to wild conclusions. Could he be doing this intentionally to be near me? I couldn't help but steal a few glances, noticing that he, too, was stealing glances in my direction.

It was as if time stood still, and in those stolen moments, I became captivated by the beauty of his gaze. His eyes locked with mine, and I couldn't help but believe that my eyes held an exquisite quality, delighting him to the point where he could gaze into them for hours without blinking.

23

A Battle of Hearts: Confronting Love and Tradition

15 July 2010

The next few days seemed to stretch endlessly, with my family members desperately trying to sit me down and discuss my decision. The conversations that unfolded were nothing short of painful. Awkwardness hung like a heavy cloud, and my heart ached with every word spoken.

It pained me deeply to realise that something as simple as having a boyfriend could elicit strong reactions from my family. The weight of their words bore down on me as they spoke of tarnished family images and the constraints of our caste. I endured the barrage of criticism and judgment that filled the air for three agonising days.

Finally, I could take no more. Fueled by determination, I mustered the courage to speak up. "This is my final decision, "I will only match with Ridhaan, I declared, hoping my family would understand and respect my choice. But alas, I was mistaken.

In an instant, the atmosphere shifted. Sitting near me, my mother lashed out and delivered a resounding slap across my face. Shock and disbelief coursed through my veins as her hand touched my cheek. It was as if the very foundation of our relationship had crumbled before my eyes.

Stunned into silence, I struggled to comprehend the severity of the situation. And then, my maternal uncle's voice cut through the tense air like a knife. "Stand up and go to your father's house; now you won't be here anymore," he coldly declared, his words hanging heavy with finality.

As tears welled in my eyes, I realised the magnitude of the moment. This was the home I had known since childhood, where I had grown up without my mom and dad. And now, I was being forced to leave, cast aside by the people who were supposed to love and support me.

There was nothing left to say. I quietly gathered my belongings and walked out of the house, the weight of their rejection etched into my soul. I went to my mother's house, seeking solace in the only place I had left to call home.

$$\triangleright\triangleright\triangleright$$

18 July 2010

Three long and arduous days had passed since I arrived at my father's house. And today, on the third day, a sombre presence again entered my life. My Nani, burdened by remorse, arrived at my father's doorstep. Her eyes glistened with tears as she apologised on my uncle's behalf.

Unable to witness her sorrow, I let go of past grievances and embraced the fleeting moments of reconciliation. Forgiveness washed over me instantly, and I decided to accompany them.

During my stay at my father's house, my mother had taken it upon herself to obtain Ridhaan's phone number from my cell. From that day forward, she made it a habit to call him repeatedly, hurling insults and abuse to force him to leave me. It seemed that Ridhaan's day now commenced with the bitter sound of my mother's harsh words.

But despite the barrage of negativity, Ridhaan remained steadfast and silent. He understood the depth of my mother's emotions and chose to respect her, even in the face of her cruel words. I truly admired this quality in him - his ability to remain composed and compassionate, even in the most trying of circumstances.

ᗷᗷᗷ

1 October 2010

Everything seemed to be going against me. College was over, and Ridhaan's business needed to be thriving. But the most frustrating part was my family's lack of support for my love life. Every week, a new suitor would come to see me, and every time, I found myself disliking the guy. Each rejection led to confrontations between our families, causing tension and chaos. This had been going on for three long months until one fateful day when my mother and Nani lost their temper and slapped me repeatedly.

"What the hell do you see in him?" they shouted angrily as their hands landed on my cheeks.

With my face burning and tears welling up, I snapped back, "I will only marry him!" and rushed to my room, locking myself inside.

ᗷᗷᗷ

Next Day
   (2 October 2010)

The following day, "Maasi" came into my room carrying a dinner plate. She sat down next to me and looked at me with concern, a string of questions forming in her mind. She gestured with a small bite of food, her eyes filled with curiosity and confusion.

"Why does he want to marry you?" she asked, her tone gentle yet full of curiosity.

"Why didn't you find a guy from our circle?" she continued, her eyebrows furrowing in perplexity.

"Was it because of this guy that you rejected the others?" she inquired, trying to understand my thought process.

"What is it about him that makes you want to marry him? Couldn't you find those qualities in an eligible bachelor from our community?" she probed further, her questions sincere yet challenging.

"What if he changes his mind after marriage? Have you thought about that?" she asked, her worry evident.

"What will our family say about you? They might ruin your image," she pointed out, her concern for my reputation palpable.

"Didn't you feel ashamed before getting into this relationship?" she questioned, seeking to understand my perspective. "And what about your siblings? They might follow in your footsteps and bring shame to our family," she added, contemplating the potential consequences.

I listened to her questions, taking in each word as I enjoyed the dinner she had brought. It had been a while since I had eaten anything cooked by her loving hands. She continued, her voice filled with a mix of wisdom and compassion.

"But Kumudh, you must also try to understand your family's perspective. We are not your enemies," she said, her eyes filled with genuine care. "All we want is for you to be happy for the rest of your life. We deny your choice of marriage not because we don't love you, but because we fear you might be making an immature decision. In this era of casual dating, we worry that this guy may not be suitable for you."

Maasi paused, urging me to put myself in her shoes. "Try to think about it from our point of view. We have concerns because we genuinely care about your happiness. You need to address our concerns and reassure us about your decision. If you shut us out completely, it will only hurt you. We are willing to pay the price for your stubbornness, but you will suffer the consequences."

She reminded me of our deep-rooted love and how they had raised me since I was a newborn. "We have always yearned for your well-being, which will never change as you grow older. So, please take into account our worries about this marriage. Please take our critical reviews as a way to make your own choices. As they say, 'love is blind,' but you don't have to be. Make sure you align your concerns with ours."

"Pausing for a moment", - Maasi offered her final advice. "However, if you are truly confident and willing to take on this challenge for the rest of your life, take a stand for yourself. Please give me a final yes or no. If you say yes, I will support you and convince the whole family to do the same. Take your time, Kumudh. I will stand by you in all your decisions."

Overwhelmed with emotions, I uttered, "I want to marry him. I wouldn't be happy without him, Maasi," as tears streamed down my face.

Maasi enveloped me in a warm embrace, understanding the depth of my feelings. "Okay," she whispered, offering her unconditional support.

24

Ink of Love: Crafting Our Union on Paper

1 November 2010

I had exhausted every conceivable method to persuade my family to approve our marriage. I had reached the point where I was convinced that I wouldn't marry at all. Running away was never an option for me; I wanted both sets of parents to bless our union. I allowed my parents to search for potential suitors to give it one last shot. They dismissed most of them outright, leaving only a few contenders. Throughout this process, I continued asserting that Ridhaan was the perfect match for me, far superior to any other candidate. I vowed to say yes only to him.

And then, like magic, my "Maasi" convinced my entire family to support our marriage. I couldn't fathom how she accomplished this, but it thrilled me. Finally, things started to fall into place. Ridhaan's business flourished, and, most importantly, my family embraced my desire to marry him.

Determined not to waste any more time, I picked up the phone and dialled Ridhaan's number.

***

Today, after an eternity, we all sat down for a family dinner while watching "Jab We Met." As the movie played, my family members couldn't help but compare me to Geet, played by Kareena Kapoor. They insisted that I resembled her in looks and my dramatic, mischievous, and stubborn nature.

The following week...

My parents met Ridhaan, and they instantly hit it off. They had a heartfelt conversation, getting to know the man he was. Similarly, we arranged a meeting for Ridhaan's parents with my family. As they interacted, it became clear that they, too, found him to be a wonderful person. The feeling was enchanting with his parents' approval secured, and my parents were entirely on board.

ᐅᐅᐅ

25 November 2010

As the success and outcome of our endeavours lie at the core of our hearts, my family took great care in ensuring that every factor contributing to the auspiciousness of this occasion was meticulously considered. Following the beliefs of Hindu families, selecting the perfect time, known as Muhurat, and the ideal place to conduct a significant event amplifies the likelihood of achieving the desired outcome. With numerous factors requiring thoughtful consideration before embarking on a task, it becomes crucial to prioritise the most significant ones. Indeed, timing is everything, and when you find yourself in the right place at the right time, nothing can hinder you from attaining your deepest desires.

After consulting with a learned scholar, three dates were suggested to us. Among them, my family chose the sacred date of 16th February 2011. Joy and elation surged within me, for today, my dream was about to materialise. Marriage—a bond rooted in profound origins, built on unwavering trust, adorned with the sweetness of love, navigates through life's challenges and finds solace in the benevolence of the divine.

Even as a young girl in kindergarten, I vividly recall being enthralled by the cheesy Bollywood love stories portrayed by Shah Rukh Khan (which, truth be told, I still hold a soft spot for, haha). I marvelled at the exquisite jewellery and resplendent attire adorning the bride during her wedding. Back then, I yearned to resemble those brides, to experience the enchantment of marrying the love of my life. And today, standing on the precipice of my childhood dreams, I couldn't help but feel like I had stepped into a surreal realm. The allure of married life, the opulence of jewellery, the vermilion adorning the parting of the hair, and the graceful drape of the saree have all fascinated me since childhood.

My family planned and organised the wedding, with preparations for the grand event underway. The venue was booked, and every other aspect was falling into place.

However, one crucial task remained: printing the wedding invitations.

I grew excited, knowing that each card would carry the essence of our union, a tangible symbol of love and togetherness. Each word and design was meticulously chosen to convey the grandeur and significance of this blessed event. The invitation would serve as a gateway, inviting our loved ones to witness the culmination of our journey and become partakers in the joyous celebration of our love.

As the printing presses were set in motion, the anticipation mounted. The tangible representation of our wedding was about to take shape, ushering in a new chapter in our lives. With each passing moment, the reality of our union grew stronger, bringing us closer to the day when our dreams would intertwine and we would embark on a lifelong journey together.

25

When Time Stood Still: A Mother's Battle for Life

September 2013

After a few months had passed, the weight of my growing belly became more and more apparent. Simple tasks, like reaching the bottom drawer, became a daunting challenge, a reminder of my increasing clumsiness. I longed for assistance, for someone to lend a helping hand during these moments. But alas, I found myself in solitude. Even my husband was absent. He had been spending his weekdays in Mumbai, returning only on Saturdays. When he did come home, he seemed more preoccupied with his desires, leaving me to fend for myself. No one bothered to inquire about how I was truly feeling.

This isolation, coupled with the physical discomfort, made me feel trapped in a crate. I often found myself groaning in frustration within the confines of my room. I resorted to peculiar habits, such as conversing with the ceiling fan as if seeking solace in its rhythmic rotations.

Occasionally, when Ajay left his laptop at home, I would steal a few moments to watch "Chota Bheem" in my room. It offered a temporary escape, a brief respite from my solitude. When my data ran out, I turned to my baby for company. Speaking softly, I used to engage in a heartfelt conversation with the little life growing inside me, my baby bump.

Gently placing my hands on my belly, I smile for hours. "Hello there, my little one. It's just you and me in this room, our little world. Can you hear me? I hope you can feel the love and warmth I'm sending you."

As I continued to speak, the walls seemed to absorb my words as if they were witnesses to this intimate moment. The bed gave me a soft and supportive foundation as I poured my heart out to my unborn child. And the fan above gently whirred, casting a comforting breeze that seemed to caress them both.

"I want you to know, my precious baby, that you are a gift beyond measure. Despite my challenges, I am filled with joy, knowing I will be your mother. You motivate me to keep going and pushing forward even when life feels difficult."

Emotionally, my voice quivered as I shared my dreams and hopes with my baby. "I promise to protect you and provide you with everything I have. I will be there for you, guiding you and showering you with love every step of the way. You are the greatest blessing in my life, and I can't wait to hold you in my arms."

I felt a fluttering sensation as if my baby had acknowledged my words. It brought tears of happiness to my eyes. "Oh, my little one, I can't wait to see your face, to witness the miracle of your existence. We will face whatever challenges come our way, and together, we will conquer them."

Despite the challenges, I consciously tried to maintain a semblance of happiness for my baby's sake. Every day, I reminded myself that my well-being directly impacted the well-being of my precious creation.

In light of this newfound responsibility, I started to prioritise self-care. Rest became necessary, and I indulged in as much sleep as my body required. However, nourishing food became a luxury I could no longer afford. The quality of my meals had deteriorated, leaving me with a sense of dissatisfaction. Nevertheless, I found solace when my mother-in-law dutifully provided me with meals, and I gratefully consumed them. It was not a matter of choice but rather a reflection of my dedication to the well-being of my unborn child.

ᐅᐅᐅ

20 December 2013

My water broke overnight as I peacefully slept, marking the arrival of my baby. At 37 weeks pregnant, my husband and in-laws hurriedly whisked me away to the hospital in an auto. Little did I know that this journey would be accompanied by an unexpected passenger: my mother-in-law.

As we squeezed ourselves into the backseat of the auto, a mix of anticipation and discomfort filled the confined space. My contractions began to intensify, adding to the already tense atmosphere. My husband tried to navigate the chaotic city streets while comforting me through the waves of pain. Meanwhile, my mother-in-law sat beside me with no worry etched across her face.

The auto jolted and swerved through the traffic, each bump magnifying my discomfort. In between contractions,

I couldn't help but steal glances at my mother-in-law, attempting to decipher her thoughts. Her presence, though unexpected, had a certain weight to it. I wondered if she was contemplating the impending expenses, a cloud of concern lingering in her mind.

As the auto trudged on, the air inside became heavy with hope, apprehension, and unspoken tensions.

Finally, the hospital came into view, a beacon of relief and medical expertise. The auto screeched to a halt, and my husband hurriedly helped me out, supported by the ever-watchful gaze of my mother-in-law.

*****

Hours later, after a painful and challenging attempt at a vaginal birth, the situation took a turn for the worse. The baby's heart rate dropped, and the excruciating part was that I felt no pain at all.

As our heart rates dipped dangerously low, I found myself connected to an oxygen supply. My baby was distressed and ready to appear, but the progress was hindered at 10 centimetres. Amid the chaos, I recall my doctor uttering words of encouragement mixed with concern, saying something like, "You're doing okay, Mommy, but the situation doesn't look good." The urgency escalated, and I was swiftly rushed to the operating room for an emergency C-section as the doctors struggled to detect the baby's heartbeat.

Amidst the commotion, I could hear my mother-in-law's murmurs. Her thoughts seemed consumed by the potential expenses. I couldn't help but suspect she might refuse to allow the doctors to proceed with the operation due to the anticipated high costs. Alternatively, she might reluctantly agree, only to later demand the money from my parents.

After what felt like an eternity...

"What the fuck is this old lady blabbering about?" I thought to myself, gritting my teeth and pushing through the pain. My agonising cries filled the room until, finally, after what felt like an eternity, the medical team rushed in.

"As I was wheeled into the operating room, the OB/GYN team had Reggaeton blasting in the background. However, seeking a calmer atmosphere, I requested a playlist of Shahrukh Khan's songs," I reminisced. Dil Chahe Jitna Pyar Utna Maang Lo... Ho, Tumko Milega Utna Pyar Main Hoon Na

A little while later, amidst their congratulatory words, I was still disoriented, wondering what they were celebrating. Suddenly, the moment arrived and out came my baby. I had hoped for that precious skin-to-skin contact and the sound of his cry. I heard the baby's screams, and my memory faded from that point onward. However, my son was born healthy, weighing 8 pounds and 10 ounces.

A few minutes passed, and as they stitched me up, I couldn't help but inquire about my baby's whereabouts. The doctor assured me that he was with his father. They all eagerly exclaimed, "Just wait until you see his eyelashes!" I impatiently yearned to see and hold him, but I had to wait for what felt like an eternity, nearly two hours.

"There was a twinge of pain from not having that immediate skin-to-skin contact, but ultimately, what mattered was that the baby was safe and sound. You do whatever it takes for the baby to arrive, and that's all that counts," I reflected.

Finally, after what felt like an eternity...

The journey had just begun, and my life was about to transform profoundly. Holding my baby for the first time, I couldn't help but feel overwhelmed with emotion. Tears streamed down my face as I cradled him close to my chest.

"You nearly took my breath away," I whispered amidst my tears, marvelling at his softness. "I've felt alone for the past few years, but now, you'll be with me. And I hope my in-laws will embrace me as their daughter after you, dear."

Time ticked on and after two long hours...

As they wheeled me into my room in the maternity ward, the effects of anaesthesia started to wear off, and a throbbing sensation emanated from my incision. To alleviate the discomfort, they administered morphine, leaving me groggy but allowing me to find solace in sleep. Oddly enough, the fear of venturing to the bathroom made me somewhat grateful for the haze. Throughout the night, I was roused every three or four hours for temperature checks—an unexpected interruption to the much-needed rest I required for my recovery.

26
Embracing Motherhood's Beautiful Chaos

December 21, 2013

The nurse gingerly removed the catheter the next day, a wave of relief washing over me as I anticipated the freedom of movement. With cautious steps, I ventured towards the bathroom, my heart pounding with anticipation and trepidation. But what greeted me was beyond anything I had expected. Shock surged through me as I witnessed the crimson tide that mingled with my urine, staining the porcelain in a grotesque display. A chilling realisation washed over me—this was far more blood than I had anticipated. Panic threatened to consume me, but the nurse's reassuring words penetrated the fog of fear.

"It's normal," she assured me, her voice a beacon of solace amidst the storm. "Many women experience bleeding for the first few days after giving birth. It's unrelated to your c-section and should taper off soon."

Relief coursed through my veins, tempering the initial shock. As I glanced down, my eyes travelled to the maxi pad, now saturated with evidence of my body's healing process. The once pristine white fabric, imbued with pink and brown hues, was now a testament to motherhood's endurance. It was a messy reminder of the physical toll I had paid to bring new life into the world.

Amidst the crimson chaos, a peculiar yellowish discharge mingled with the blood, adding an unexpected twist to this postpartum journey. It was a strange sight, an unwelcome guest in an already turbulent landscape. Yet, amidst the discomfort and uncertainty, I clung to the knowledge that this, too, shall pass.

However, it wasn't just the physical challenges that plagued me in these early days. Navigating the demands of my newborn felt like traversing a minefield, each step wrought with anxiety and uncertainty. The sheer weight of responsibility settled heavily on my shoulders, threatening to topple me at any moment.

To compound matters, my mother-in-law, in all her well-intentioned wisdom, seemed blissfully unaware of the toll this phase took on me. She would often retreat to her slumber, relinquishing the child's care to my weary arms. It was as if she couldn't fathom the exhaustion that consumed me, the overwhelming fatigue that gripped my entire being.

Amid this struggle, I yearned for respite, for someone to share the burden of motherhood. But as the days unfolded, I realised that strength must come from within. Each passing moment became an opportunity to discover the depths of my resilience and forge a connection with my child that transcended the weariness of body and soul.

And so, with every step I took, every tear I shed, and every smile I mustered, I slowly embraced motherhood's beautiful chaos. Though the road ahead seemed daunting, I knew deep within that this journey would ultimately transform me into a stronger, more compassionate version of myself.

The struggle was real, but so was my determination. And as I gazed upon my precious child, cradled in my bare arms, I vowed to navigate this storm with unwavering love and unyielding strength.

December 22. 2013

The obsession with gas has taken hold of everyone around me. It was as if the entire world was fixated on this peculiar bodily function. Doctors and nurses, with a straight face, kept bombarding me with questions about passing gas. This seemingly mundane act was a monumental milestone, indicating that my insides were functioning again. Until then, I was condemned to a liquid diet, unable to savour the delights of solid food. So, they handed me a simple cup of tea, a feeble substitute for the culinary delights I craved.

To manage the pain, I religiously popped a painkiller every four hours. Surprisingly, it did its job quite effectively. My days were a hodgepodge of activities: slow laps around the sterile corridors of the maternity ward, moments of respite interspersed with attempts at mastering the art of breastfeeding, and stolen glances at our little bundle of joy. He wasn't particularly ravenous yet, content to sleep through most of the day. He would be whisked to the nursery in the evenings, granting me the luxury of uninterrupted rest.

But let me tell you, extricating myself from the hospital bed was a Herculean task. My mother-in-law was conveniently absent, so I devised my strategy. First, I propped myself on one elbow, summoning all my strength.

Then, with a determined push from my other arm, I gradually propelled myself forward. I soon discovered that lowering the bed to create a sharp angle where my head rested alleviated the strain on my tender incision. Walking upright felt like tugging at the stitches, so I settled for a hunched-over shuffle, my IV trailing reluctantly behind me. Astonishingly, once I set myself in motion, I realised I wasn't as feeble as I had initially thought. I could manage three laps around the maternity ward, defying the limitations of my recovering body.

December 23, 2013

I felt as though a train had mercilessly run me over. The weight of exhaustion clung to my bones, far more substantial and draining than the day prior. It dawned on me that this weariness wasn't solely a result of the surgery; it was the accumulation of all those futile pushes finally catching up to me. The desire to reach out and say hello to everyone tugged at my heart, but my energy was so depleted that even picking up the phone seemed insurmountable.

Finally, after enduring five seemingly endless days, I was granted leave from the hospital. The anticipation of freedom mingled with a lingering sense of weakness as if the ordeal had extracted every ounce of strength from within me. Slowly, I gathered my belongings, each step an arduous task, and made my way toward the exit.

As I ventured outside, a cool winter breeze brushed against my face, gently reminding me that life continued beyond the sterile walls of the hospital. I inhaled deeply, relishing the fresh air filling my lungs, and allowed a faint smile to grace my lips. The possibilities that awaited me outside these confines seemed both exhilarating and overwhelming..

27

Echoes of Silence

14 December 2010

The whirlwind pace at which everything was falling into place overwhelmed me. My dad had contacted Ridhaan and his father to discuss the engagement arrangements and logistics. As the day arrived, tensions lingered, and I was caught in a storm of emotions.

It was 8 PM when Ridhaan and his father entered our home. They were led into the drawing room, where my family awaited their arrival. Meanwhile, I busied myself in the kitchen, preparing a meal for our families, side by side with my mother. The aroma of spices filled the air, intermingling with the brewing storm of anticipation.

After a few moments, unable to resist the urge, I crept closer to the drawing room to eavesdrop on their conversation. My heart sank as I overheard Ridhaan's father audaciously demand a dowry of ten lakh rupees. The words hung in the air, and I turned my attention to Ridhaan himself, hoping for a reaction that would reassure me.

To my surprise, Ridhaan sat there, seemingly unperturbed by his father's demand. Disbelief washed over me. "What is he doing? How can he sit there so nonchalantly?" I thought to myself, my mind racing with anger and confusion. I had always believed Ridhaan's family was different, that they valued our relationship above material possessions. But this demand shattered my illusions.

"Come on, Ridhaan, stand up for us. Stand up for our love," I silently pleaded, feeling the weight of disappointment settle upon my heart.

(I'll skip the part where my father and maternal uncle had almost agreed to pay the dowry, going against their long-held beliefs.)

Dowry has always been a contentious issue for me. I despised those who gave dowries, believing it diminished a woman's worth and perpetuated inequality. But today, faced with the prospect of my family resorting to it, my perspective wavered. I couldn't hate them, for I understood they were doing it out of love and the desire for my happiness. The conflict within me deepened.

"You accept bribes from the bride's family to marry your son. By doing so, you are devaluing the bride and turning her into a commodity," I found myself silently accusing Ridhaan's family. Their demand for ten lakh rupees only served to strengthen this conviction. I couldn't help but question Ridhaan's capabilities. If he needed his wife to bring in money for him, did that mean he couldn't earn it himself? The thought was disheartening, leaving me questioning his worthiness as a partner. Even his parents should feel ashamed of their son and themselves.

Marriage, in its essence, is a sacred bond that refines love and respect. It is a ritual that holds meaning and significance and is revered by society. Yet Ridhaan and his family insulted these genuine relationships and sacred rituals by reducing them to financial transactions.

As I stood there, grappling with my conflicted emotions, I couldn't help but wonder how this revelation would affect our relationship. Once a joyful occasion, the engagement had now become tainted by the shadows of greed and compromise. Would Ridhaan find the strength to break free from these shackles and reaffirm our love? Or would the echoes of his silence be the final verdict on our journey together?

Only time would reveal the answers hidden within our hearts and the path we would ultimately choose.

28

Silent Whispers: Seeking the Name of Fate

(30 December 2013)

Exhausted from the challenges of post-pregnancy and the lack of support from my in-laws and Ajay, I shouldered all the responsibilities for our child. Even my stitches hadn't healed properly, yet my in-laws and Ajay seemed oblivious to my struggles. However, today was different. They all suddenly showed concern and care, perhaps prompted by the presence of my beloved family members—my Nani, my sister, and my Maasi.

Amidst the preparations for the Naam Karan ceremony, an essential event in our Hindu tradition, I couldn't help but reflect on the significance of choosing the perfect name for our son. We Hindus believe that a child's name holds the power to shape his destiny and influence his character. The alignment of the planets at the time of birth is considered crucial, as an incompatible name can invite misfortune. Naturally, I wanted the best for my little one, so selecting the right name became important.

As discussions unfolded, suggestions for names starting with the letter "H" poured in from every corner. Friends, relatives, and even scholars offered their ideas, each with their reasoning and significance attached. However, I needed more than the suggested names to resonate with me. It felt like something was missing—something that would truly capture the essence of my son's unique identity.

Curious about my decision, the scholar turned to me and asked, "So, have you decided on a name?"

I paused momentarily, taking in the weight of this decision, and replied, "I will reveal the chosen name in due time."

Little did they know, I had been silently exploring many possibilities, searching for a name that would embody the beauty and potential within my precious child. It was a name that needed to reflect his strengths, aspirations, and the boundless love he brought into our lives. And until I found that perfect name, I would patiently wait, guided by a mother's intuition and a heart full of hope.

29

Love Beyond Dowry

15 December 2011

From childhood, I had dreamt of a love marriage, just like Geet from "Jab We Met," played by Kareena Kapoor. Little did I know that life would imitate art, and I would find myself in a situation similar to Kareena's character.

With a heavy heart, I made a decision and called Ridhaan the next day. My words were filled with sadness and determination.

"Your name, Ridhaan, means 'someone is in search of something.' Initially, I believed you were searching for love in me, but it seems that what you truly seek is wealth."

The weight of disappointment lingered in the air as I continued, "I am calling off this wedding. The family who once promised that they wanted only me as their daughter-in-law has changed their stance, demanding ten lakh rupees as dowry. I am staunchly against dowry and refuse to 'buy' a man and a family who don't honour their word. Therefore, I have made the difficult decision to cancel this wedding."

There was a moment of disbelief and confusion on the other end of the line, "What? You're revoking the marriage?

But you gave your word," Ankit interjected.

Sighing heavily, I replied, my voice laden with sadness, "Yes, I have cancelled my wedding because of dowry. However, the details of this decision should not be measured or justified. What matters most is the overwhelming wave of relief that washed over me when I considered cancelling my nuptials. This was not a decision made in haste or without careful consideration. There were numerous emotions to navigate, difficult conversations to endure, and heart-wrenching questions and answers to confront. Yet, amidst it all, I clung to the relief I felt and took one step at a time."

Cancelling a wedding, especially one that has been eagerly anticipated, is stressful and frightening. It feels like standing on a platform as a train hurtles toward you. The pressure to marry Ridhaan, my beloved, was immense, and I had gone to great lengths to make it happen.

Yet, deep within, I knew that cancelling this marriage was the right thing to do, despite it being a step towards correcting my mistakes. The thought of continuing with a union tainted by the demand for dowry was unbearable.

"And finally, this marriage is cancelled," I concluded, my voice cracking sorrowfully. "I am distressed because I loved Ridhaan more than my life."

Tears welled in my eyes as I hung up the phone, and my heart ached with a profound sense of loss. The dreams I had built around this relationship were shattered, and the pain of letting go gnawed at my soul. But somewhere within me, I held onto a glimmer of hope that someday, I would find the love and respect I deserved, free from the chains of dowry and false promises.

30
Whispers of Fate

December 2016 (train)

Morning broke through the train windows, casting a soft golden glow over the compartments. The rhythmic chugging of the engine resonated in the air, harmonising with the murmur of sleepy passengers. It was a tranquil scene, the perfect setting for a chance encounter that would soon turn my world upside down.

As the train drew nearer to his station, anticipation buzzed. The minutes felt like an eternity, each second ticking slowly. And then, just as the world outside blurred past, he reached into his pocket, pulling out a small piece of paper. There was a flicker of uncertainty in his eyes as if he were contemplating the consequences of his next action. Little did I know then that that slip of paper held secrets yet to be unveiled.

He handed it to me with a subtle smile and said, "I know this is probably creepy, but here's my number." His words hung in the air, a daring invitation that caught me off guard. It was an audacious move, an unexpected twist in the ordinary routine of life.

Caught up in the moment, I met his gaze, a mix of surprise and curiosity painting my expression. "Sometimes, you just gotta pull the trigger!" I responded, a rush of excitement pulsating through me. Our eyes locked briefly as if sharing a secret language only we could understand. And then, he turned his attention to my son, Aarav, offering him a sweet toffee, a small act of kindness that revealed a glimpse of his character.

As the train slowed to a halt at his stop, he bid us farewell, stepping out onto the platform. I watched him fade into the distance, a pang of anticipation lingering. In my hand, I clutched that little piece of paper, holding the key to a future that seemed both exhilarating and uncertain.

I peered down at the paper, my heart racing as I deciphered his name: Dr Arjun Singh. His profession seemed to whisper promises of mystery and intrigue, while his number promised a connection yet to be explored. His handwriting, a testament to the age-old stereotype of doctors and their notorious scrawl, added a touch of charm to the whole encounter.

Determined, I folded the paper and held it close, a vow to keep it safe. "Whatever you do, do not lose this!" I reminded myself, feeling a warmth rise in my cheeks. The rest of the journey passed in a blur as my mind replayed the scene over and over, unable to fully grasp the reality of what had transpired. I was enveloped in a bubble of excitement, oblivious to the gazes of fellow passengers who had witnessed our unexpected exchange. At that moment, their curious eyes were inconsequential, overshadowed by the thrill of the unknown.

I decided to take the plunge that night, unable to contain my curiosity any longer. I picked up my phone, my fingers hovering over the screen. With a nervous smile, I typed out a message and pressed send. The message disappeared into the digital realm with a hint of vulnerability and the promise of a new beginning. The night held its breath, waiting for a reply determining the course of our intertwined destinies.

31
The Weight of Silence

December 16, 2010

The weight of depression descended upon me after the cancellation of my marriage, consuming me from the inside out. It felt like an insidious monster had occupied my mind, gradually eroding my sense of self. Despite the unwavering support of my family and friends, I couldn't escape the overwhelming loneliness that enveloped me. It was as if I were utterly alone in a people-filled room.

Ojas, my only college friend after Riya and Ridhaan, started coming to my home more frequently, attempting to offer solace amid my despair. But no matter what words were spoken to me, my mind twisted them into something negative. I had become my worst enemy, constantly berating myself and finding fault in every situation. The incessant chatter in my head drained me of all energy, leaving me yearning for respite, even if it meant seeking refuge in sleep and waking up felt like a nightmare because it meant facing another day of the same torment.

Nighttime became particularly daunting as the voices in my head amplified their discordant symphony. The fear that gripped me at the thought of sleeplessness intensified my frustration. Insomnia and depression seemed to intertwine, trapping me in a relentless cycle of restlessness and exhaustion.

Deep down, I knew I needed help, but the act of reaching out for it weighed heavily on my already burdened heart. Asking for assistance made me feel like a weight, a burden on those around me. So, I retreated into the confines of my room, spending hours in tearful solitude, reliving the memories I once cherished with Ridhaan.

A doctor was summoned daily to check on me, their visits a stark reminder of my deteriorating state. The dizziness had become my constant companion, causing me to stumble and falter with each step I took.

Amidst the chaos in my mind, I yearned for freedom. I craved liberation from the clutches of medications, doctors, counsellors, hospitals, and the suffocating darkness of negative thoughts. It felt like I had lost a vital part of myself, and the notion of ever being whole again seemed elusive. Motivation eluded me, for how could I envision a future without Ridhaan by my side?

Anxiety intertwined itself with my every thought, leading me to doubt the authenticity of the love offered by those around me. The words "cheer up" became a trigger, unleashing a torrent of tormenting thoughts. I blamed myself for failing to conceal the depth of my despair from those who cared about me.

Although I longed for someone to understand my pain, I couldn't summon the courage to voice it aloud. Even now, my communication with "Maasi" remains strained, as I find solace only in the solitude of my room. In my isolation, I believed that shutting myself off from the world would prevent any further harm from befalling me.

But deep down, a glimmer of hope flickered, a small voice whispering that there might still be a way out of the labyrinthine darkness that had consumed me.

32

Shadows of Desperation

16 February 2011

The clock struck 6 PM, and tears had been streaming down my face since the previous night. I couldn't forget what had happened to me. And today, of all days, was the wretched culmination of my pain. Anguish filled my heart as I cursed whatever divine force had played a hand in altering the course of my life.

***

7 PM

I found myself locked away in the confines of my room, drowning in a sea of despair. The weight of my depression pressed heavily upon me, suffocating my every thought. My family, aware of my torment, kept a watchful eye on me, never letting me stray far from their sight except in the bathroom. They would stand at the doorway, their ears attuned to the slightest hint of trouble, even during those private moments.

I entered the bathroom, wearing my long-sleeved cardigan, and closed the door behind me. In that solitary space, my mind wandered to dark places. As a desperate test of my strength, I removed the cardigan and tightly wound it around my neck, pulling at it slightly. It was an unsettling experiment, a morbid curiosity to see if I had the physical capability to end my own life. I realised that, at that moment, I possessed the means to do it, but a glimmer of something within me held me back.

Struggling to remove the tangled fabric, panic began to consume me. I hastily pulled the cardigan over my head, trying not to arouse suspicion by staying in the bathroom for too long. Once neatly styled, my hair appeared dishevelled, reflecting the turmoil that ravaged my soul. With as much composure as I could muster, I smoothed my hair, completed my tasks in the bathroom, and emerged.

As I washed my hands, my "Maasi" observed me with a watchful eye. Perhaps she noticed the slight disarray of my hair or the fact that I carried my cardigan in a bundle rather than wearing it. Yet, after all they had witnessed, my family understood that sometimes all they needed to do was wait, knowing that I would eventually reveal my actions without prompting. They understood me in ways I didn't even understand myself.

Moments later, I approached "Maasi" again, my voice trembling as I asked for a private conversation. I cautiously explained what I had done, attempting to downplay the severity of my actions. There was a hint of sternness in her response, but it was not devoid of empathy. There was danger in her words, as if she wanted to jolt me out of my perilous situation and make me confront the reality of my circumstances.

As our conversation progressed, a wave of overwhelming emotions washed over me. Bent over, I covered my face, succumbing to uncontrollable sobs. Surprisingly, "Maasi" spoke with a tenderness I never expected to hear from her. Softly, she said, "It's okay." Her voice carried understanding as if she could fathom the depths of my pain. She continued, "I don't believe you truly want to die. It seems you're trapped in excruciating agony and seeking an escape. Am I correct?" I could only manage a nod in response. Her words struck a chord within me; she accurately captured the essence of my torment.

At that moment, as I had wrapped the cardigan around my neck, testing the limits of my existence, I felt as though I had nothing left to lose. But now, as I reflect upon those dark thoughts, I understand the truth. To die by suicide would mean forfeiting everything and relinquishing my life and the potential for change and growth. It is not merely suicide; it is the murder of a new generation of thought, the demise of a woman whose worth is reduced to a ten-day spectacle orchestrated by a culture and community that thrives on falsehoods.

The battle between my inner demons and the fragile flicker of hope within me raged on, intensifying my struggle with each passing day.

33

Embracing the Sunrise of Freedom

January 1, 2014

The weight of my burdens was unbearable, pressing down on me with each passing day. It felt as though the world had conspired against me, painting my life with shades of agony and humiliation. The physical toll on my body was evident, with the unsightly bruises adorning my most intimate parts as a constant reminder of my pain. Even worse, the cruel jests from my "in-laws" seemed to haunt me at every turn, shredding any remnants of self-esteem I had left.

Escape became my only solace. I yearned to spread my wings and soar away from this suffocating environment. However, the oppressive atmosphere returned, with Nani, my sister, and "Maasi" no longer present, suffusing the air with toxicity. It was suffocating, driving me to the brink of madness.

On New Year's, the entire family, my in-laws, embarked on a joyous celebration for the new year. Little did they know, they left me imprisoned within the walls of our home, a living testament to their disregard for my happiness and freedom. The loneliness and isolation consumed me, leaving me feeling like a caged bird, unable to spread my wings and find respite in the world outside.

Days passed, and the news of my mistreatment reached the ears of my Mama and Nani. They wasted no time contacting Ajay and confronting him about the unpleasant revelations they had stumbled upon during the Naam Karan ceremony. As their concern weighed heavily on my heart, I was torn between loyalty to my family and the desperate need for liberation.

Then, a lifeline appeared in the form of my beloved "Maasi," a figure who had always been my pillar of strength. I saw her voice's glimmer of truth and understanding as she urged me to reveal the reality of my in-laws' treatment on the call. I wanted to protect her, shield her from the harsh reality, but the lies I had woven around myself began to unravel.

"I'm fine, Maasi," I uttered weakly, the words barely escaping my trembling lips. It was the same old refrain, the lie I had mastered perfectly. But her persistence, unwavering love and concern were too powerful to resist. She had seen through the facade, witnessed the agony etched onto my every fibre.

I could no longer bear the weight of my deceptions. The dam broke, and the truth spilt forth like a torrential downpour. My voice quivered with relief and anguish as I confessed my torment. The depression that had gripped my soul was laid bare, the depths of my despair exposed.

At that moment, as the words tumbled out, I felt a sliver of hope. By embracing the truth, I could begin to heal. It was a small step that held the promise of liberation from the darkness threatening to consume me whole.

ᐯᐯᐯ

January 13, 2014

We spoke for 2 hours; I poured out my heart and shared my deepest fears. Every word carried the weight of my anguish as I confided in "Maasi," seeking solace and understanding. But as I concluded our conversation, my heart sank, knowing that the respite I found in our words would soon be shattered as the heavy silence of the room was abruptly broken by the jarring sound of my father-in-law wrenching open the door. His face contorted with fury, and he unleashed a barrage of abusive words, each piercing my already fragile state of mind. I could feel the weight of his disappointment, his disapproval, crushing me with every syllable. It was as if he had heard every word I had uttered to "Maasi" and found them utterly repugnant.

Before I could recover from the shock of his verbal assault, my mother-in-law joined in, her voice adding another layer of condemnation. The echoes of their accusations reverberated in my mind, amplifying the despair that had taken root within me. I fought to maintain my composure and a semblance of control, but the dam holding back my emotions was crumbling rapidly.

In those agonising moments, I felt the walls closing in on me, suffocating any glimmer of hope that remained. The weight of their collective judgment, their relentless disapproval, pushed me to my breaking point. The dam burst, and I found myself shouting and shrieking, releasing the pent-up anguish that had consumed me for far too long.

As the chaos unfolded, a wave of concerned acquaintances rushed to the scene, their bewildered faces mirroring their bewilderment at the eruption of emotions. They sought to understand what had transpired, their inquiries blending into a cacophony of voices.

Amidst the chaos, I pleaded for Ajay to hear my side of the story and to believe in my truth. But to my dismay, he seemed to side with his parents, casting doubt upon my every word.

The rejection and disbelief from Ajay shattered the remnants of my fragile spirit. I felt abandoned and alone in my struggle. The injustice I felt ignited a fire of anger within me. In desperation, I reached out to my Mama, the one person I believed could offer me an escape from this suffocating environment.

"I can't bear this any longer," I whispered hoarsely into the phone, trembling with fear and defiance. "Come here, please. Please take me away from this torment, this unbearable pain. If you don't, I'll have no choice but to disappear into the unknown."

As I uttered those words, a heavy silence enveloped me once more; only this time, it carried the weight of my shattered dreams and a profound sense of desolation. The phone call ended, leaving me in despair, waiting for a lifeline, a glimmer of hope to guide me out of the darkness that threatened to consume me entirely.

*****

Mama called Ajay to have a serious conversation. Ajay recounted the distressing events that had unfolded recently in a confident voice. He described how I was behaving with his parents and had been like a bitch.

"Please," Ajay implored, his voice laden with emotion. "Teach her how to treat my parents. Help her understand the love and respect they deserves."

Understanding the gravity of the situation, Mama reassured him, "Don't worry. We will come and take Kumud with us for a few days.

January 15, 2014

The morning sun cast a warm, golden glow through the curtains, gently awakening me from a restless sleep. A glimmer of hope ignited within my weary heart as I lay there, listening to the sweet symphony of birdsong outside my window. Today was the first ray of light breaking through the darkness that had enveloped me in this oppressive place - my in-laws' house, the epitome of my hell.

With anticipation and nervousness, I rose from the bed and took a deep breath, inhaling the scent of freedom that seemed to linger in the air. The walls of this suffocating place, which had witnessed my silent tears and stifled cries, would soon become a distant memory. Today, my family members were coming to rescue me, to liberate me from the chains that had bound me for far too long.

As I moved through the house, memories of the torment I had endured flashed before my eyes: the disparaging remarks, the endless expectations, and the constant feeling of being an outsider in a world that had never fully embraced me. But today, as I gathered my belongings and carefully packed them into suitcases, a newfound sense of empowerment surged through my veins. I was reclaiming my life, reclaiming my voice.

The excitement was mixed with a tinge of apprehension as I imagined the forthcoming reunion with my family. Would they understand the depths of my suffering? Would they be able to see the scars that adorned my spirit, the wounds inflicted by years of emotional imprisonment? I longed for their unconditional love and support, yearning for the warmth of their embrace, hoping that I would find the strength to heal in their presence.

As the final item was carefully placed in my suitcase, I took one last look around the room that had witnessed my silent struggles. It was as if the walls themselves held echoes of my pain, but today they would no longer confine me. Today, I would step out into the world a survivor, ready to embark on a journey of self-discovery and liberation.

The doorbell rang, breaking through the moment of reflection. My heart skipped a beat as I hurriedly approached the front door. Opening it, I was met with tear-filled eyes and outstretched arms, a testament to the love and unwavering support that awaited me on the other side. My family, my lifeline, stood before me, ready to lead me back to a life filled with love, acceptance, and the promise of brighter days.

With a mixture of gratitude and relief, I took one final glance at the house that had held me captive for so long. Today, I was breaking free, leaving behind the suffocating shadows to embrace the sunlight that beckoned me forward. And as I crossed the threshold, a sense of liberation washed over me, filling every fibre of my being. The journey to rebuild my shattered spirit had just begun, and with my family by my side, I knew I could finally leave behind the painful chapters of my past and create a future filled with hope, joy, and the unyielding strength of my resilience.

34

Destiny's Embrace

15 January 2017

I texted him that night, my fingers trembling with anticipation. The digital world became our bridge, connecting two souls hungry for companionship. After a month of exchanging heartfelt messages, baring my soul to Arjun—now known as Dr. Arjun—I felt a sense of relief. He knew every intricacy of my past relationships and even the joys and challenges of being a mother.

What amazed me most was Arjun's unwavering acceptance of my son, a gesture that deepened my admiration for him. Despite not meeting in person, our distance seemed insignificant compared to the profound bond we had forged. Arjun resided in Indore while I was nestled in another city, but plans for a physical encounter were already set in motion.

One evening, as the melodic notes of "Dekha Hazaroo Dafaa Apko," my new ringtone reverberated through the air, and my heart leapt with excitement. It was Arjun calling. Every nerve in my body tingled with anticipation as I answered the call.

I: "Hey! What's up?"

Arjun: "Nothing much. Just visited Dr Ambedkar's birthplace."

I: "Really? How did that happen? It's in Mhow."

Arjun: "Well, that's where I am, too."

I couldn't believe my ears. The elation within me surged, making it challenging to find the right words. I closed my eyes, allowing my imagination to run wild, painting vivid pictures of what it would be like to be with Arjun finally.

A moment of silence hung in the air, pregnant with anticipation.

Arjun: "So?"

I: "So?"

Arjun: "So, if you're free, let's meet."

My heart skipped a beat, racing with exhilaration. The prospect of meeting Arjun in person sent ripples of excitement through my veins.

I: "Yes, sure! I'd love to meet. When and where?"

Arjun: "How about meeting for coffee? Tomorrow, around 4 PM?"

I: "That works for me. Let's do it. Good night, Arjun."

As I ended the call, a broad smile adorned my face. The thought of finally meeting Arjun filled me with uncontainable joy, tinged with a hint of nervousness. Little did I know that this meeting would coincide with the anniversary of the worst day of my life—January 16th.

Yet, the irony didn't dampen my spirits. Instead, it added an unexpected layer of significance to our rendezvous. Strangely enough, destiny seemed to conspire to bring us together on a day marked by sorrow, igniting a flicker of hope within the depths of my soul.

Despite the darkness that once enveloped me, I found solace in the newfound light of Arjun's presence. He became the beacon of hope shining through the shadows of my past. It was as if the universe had aligned our paths in mysterious ways, drawing us together to kindle a flame of love and healing on a day with such painful memories.

35

Bound by an Invisible Thread

16 January 2017

Every passing hour seemed to drag on the following day as I anxiously awaited the moment. Jitters consumed me, making it difficult to focus on anything else. After a long battle of choosing the perfect outfit, I tried on ten different dresses to see which one made me feel stunning. Finally, I settled on a delicate, light green chicken kurta, accentuating my true self. With my long, black-reddish kinky hair flowing and lipstick adorning my lips, I felt a sense of allure reminiscent of Kareena.

It was finally time around 3:45 PM. I intentionally arrived early, not wanting to keep my date waiting for our first meeting. Standing near the elevator, I felt a mixture of excitement and nervousness. Then, after a while, I heard a voice from behind.

"Kumudh?" the voice called out.

There he was. Finally, our eyes met. He had a slight beard, and his red-checkered shirt perfectly complemented his skin tone. With a sturdy watch adorning his wrist, he exuded an irresistible charm. His pleasing personality completely mesmerised me, and at that moment, I couldn't help but think how much I wanted to be close to him. However, I pushed those thoughts aside and greeted him.

"Hi, Arjun," I said, trying to contain my excitement.

Arjun greeted me warmly, and we entered the elevator together. I also glanced at myself in the elevator's mirror, catching Arjun stealing glances. Curiosity got the better of me, and I couldn't help but ask.

"Why are you measuring this place?" I inquired.

Arjun chuckled. "No reason, just passing the time, Kumudh."

As the elevator reached our destination, Arjun flashed a warm smile and gestured for me to step out first. His chivalrous gesture made my heart flutter with appreciation and admiration.

"Thank you," I replied, returning his smile and gracefully stepping out of the elevator. The air outside felt invigorating, and excitement filled the atmosphere.

Arjun followed closely behind, and delightful anticipation lingered between us as we walked. The soft murmur of our footsteps echoed in the hallway, blending harmoniously with the rhythm of our hearts.

I glanced over at Arjun, his presence magnetic and captivating. His eyes sparkled with genuine interest and care, making me feel like the most important person.

With each step we took, I could sense a deepening connection and an unspoken understanding. It was as if the world around us faded, leaving only the two bound by an invisible thread of affection.

We found a cosy middle table tucked away from the bustling crowd.

With a gentle sway of my hips, I gracefully walked towards the table, the fresh breeze caressing my skin. I turned around, my eyes locked with Arjun's, silently inviting him to join me in this new adventure.

As we settled into our seats, I couldn't help but notice how close Arjun sat beside me. The proximity sent delightful shivers down my spine, and my heart skipped a beat. Our eyes met, and a knowing smile passed between us, silently acknowledging the unspoken chemistry that was brewing.

"Listen, I feel like having some tea. What about you?" Arjun asked.

I pondered for a moment and replied, "Hmm."

"Alright, let's go to the counter together and check out the options," Arjun suggested, leading the way.

I followed closely, our bodies almost touching as we stood near the counter. As I perused the menu, our arms brushed against each other, sending a delightful shiver down my spine. In that instant, I knew I was falling for Arjune all over again.

"So, have you decided?" Arjun inquired, breaking my trance.

"I'll have a latte," I replied, somewhat distracted.

"Okay, one cappuccino and one latte, please," Arjun ordered.

We exchanged smiles as we waited for our beverages.

As the initial awkwardness faded away, we enjoyed each other's company. The conversation flowed effortlessly, and we laughed and shared stories. However, I couldn't help but notice Arjun stealing glances at my legs, his attempt at recovery laughable. Trying to diffuse the situation, I took a sip of my coffee and remarked.

"They've put the wrong names on the beverages," I pointed out.

Arjun looked over, a smile spreading across his face. "Oh, yes," he responded, "we should switch our mugs."

And at that moment, as we made this minor correction, a connection blossomed between us. I smiled as I took my first sip, stealing glances at Arjun, who seemed to share the same silly mistake. For about ten minutes, a comfortable silence enveloped us.

Feeling the need to break the silence, I gathered my thoughts and said, "This is my first date ever."

Arjun's eyes widened in surprise.

. "Oh?"

"Yes," I confirmed.

"I hope I'm not boring you," Arjun joked.

I let out a genuine laugh. Little did he know how I truly felt at that moment.

Then, Arjun opened the chapter of my life I had been waiting for. We talked for hours, diving into deep conversations and sharing our dreams, fears, and aspirations. Time seemed to stand still as we explored the depths of our hearts.

Finally, amid our conversation, Arjun asked a question that caught me off guard.

"Do you still love your ex, Ridhaan?"

Without hesitation, I replied, "No, I hate him more than my husband."

The weather had turned stunningly beautiful, and Arjun nodded, changing the topic to lighten the mood. Sensing the beautiful surroundings, I gazed outside and suggested, "Oh, can we go for a walk?"

Arjun looked intrigued and asked, "Where should we go?"

"How about a park?" I suggested, trying to come up with an idea.

"No, no. Others might mistake us for a couple and kick us out," Arjun replied.

"Really?" I exclaimed, taken aback.

"Yes, and that's exactly why I call you a kid," Arjun teased, laughter dancing in his eyes. "Let's just walk randomly."

Arjun and I stood up simultaneously. I could feel his gaze lingering on me.

With a gentle sway of my hips, I took deliberate steps towards the elevator, aware of Arjun's eyes following my every move. The knowledge of his gaze made my heart race, and a subtle blush painted my cheeks.

I glanced over my shoulder and caught a glimpse of Arjun; his eyes locked on me with an intensity that sent my pulse racing. At that moment, I realised the depth of his attraction and the magnetic connection between us.

A playful smile tugged at the corners of my lips as I continued walking, my confidence growing with each passing second. The anticipation and chemistry between us created an electric atmosphere, and I couldn't help but revel in the enchantment of the moment.

The journey to the elevator felt like a dance; our steps synchronised in perfect harmony. I savoured the fleeting glances Arjune stole, the way his eyes traced my silhouette, igniting a fire within me.

As we reached the elevator, I turned to face Arjun, our eyes locking again in a silent exchange of desire and anticipation. The elevator doors opened, inviting us into a private realm to explore our connection's depths further.

With a mischievous twinkle in his eyes, Arjun stepped forward, holding the door open for me, a gesture that spoke volumes about his consideration and admiration. I met his gaze, feeling a surge of gratitude and excitement.

I entered the elevator, feeling his presence behind me. The air was thick with unspoken words and hidden desires. The doors closed, enclosing us in a moment of suspended time, a realm where the world faded away, leaving only the two of us.

My nerves grew as I noticed Arjun doing something absurd—he was cleaning the elevator floor. In that quirky moment, he suddenly bent down.

He held my hand with a rose and said, "Happiness always comes with a pinch of darkness. The darkness comprises guilt, regret, fear, and sadness. And hence, with time, let's learn to embrace the darkness."

Those beautiful words filled my heart, and he kissed my hand, confessing, "I love you."

Overwhelmed with emotions, I struggled to find the right words to respond. But before I could speak, the elevator reached our desired floor, where people eagerly waited to enter. A gentle chime signalled the opening of the doors. The outside world beckoned, and with excitement, I stepped out, feeling a surge of anticipation coursing through me.

Arjun followed closely behind, his presence comforting and reassuring. The air outside the elevator felt refreshing, carrying a sense of possibility and adventure. We stood side by side, our eyes locked for a moment as if silently acknowledging the significance of this moment.

With a shared smile, we began walking away from the elevator, venturing into endless possibilities. Each step felt lighter, fueled by our growing connection.

As we left the elevator behind, I could feel Arjun's gaze on me, his eyes full of admiration and intrigue. It was as if he couldn't tear his eyes away, captivated by my every move. I revelled in the attention, feeling a sense of empowerment and attraction.

Walking side by side, we found ourselves on a deserted road.

I couldn't help but steal glances at Arjun. His presence beside me was magnetic, and I was drawn to his charm and genuine nature. The moments of silence were comfortable, filled with our unspoken understanding.

Let me know when you get tired. I'm pretty used to walking," I replied, breaking the silence.

Arjun looked at me playfully and said, "Why do you always have to hurt my male ego?" He winked mischievously, and we both laughed.

"Oh, there's a pharmacy across the road. Just wait here. I'll quickly go and come back," Arjun informed me.

"No, no. Why should I stay here? I'll come with you. What do you need, anyway?" I asked curiously.

"Condoms," Arjun responded, his face maintaining a severe expression.

I froze in terror, my mind racing with disbelief. "What the...?" I thought to myself.

"I have a cold," Arjun said, bursting into laughter.

Relief washed over me, and I playfully scolded him, saying, "Oh, you scared the hell out of me! Let me come with you."

"Why do you have to bother? Just wait here. I'll be back soon," Arjun insisted.

"I'm scared of being alone. Happy now? Let's cross the road together," I said, determined not to let him go alone.

As we continued our journey, the path led us to a bustling bus stop, where people hurriedly moved about, each with their destinations in mind. The anticipation of our next adventure filled the air, and we stood side by side, awaiting the bus's arrival.

Amidst the crowd, I couldn't help but steal glances at Arjun, my heart fluttering with excitement and contentment. His presence beside me brought a sense of warmth and security, and I cherished the moments we shared in this seemingly ordinary yet significant setting.

Arjun shifted momentarily to his phone, checking messages and notifications as we stood there. Observing his focus, I couldn't help but smile, realising that even amidst the chaos, he still tried to stay connected with the world while valuing our time together.

I watched Arjun engrossed in his phone, admiring his dedication and multitasking abilities. In these small moments, I discovered new layers to his personality, deepening my affection for him even further.

As the minutes ticked by, I glanced at the approaching buses, contemplating the possibilities. The vibrant atmosphere of the bus stop mirrors the excitement and energy that thrived within our budding relationship.

Our connection remained palpable between the murmurs of conversations and the sound of engines. We exchanged glances, sharing unspoken sentiments that only intensified the bond we were building. At that moment, the world around us seemed to fade away, leaving only the two of us enveloped in a cocoon of love and anticipation.

The song "Aankhe teri kitni hasi" played softly in the background, intensifying the romantic ambience. I turned away but could feel the sparks of love connecting me to Arjun.

Our eyes met, and we exchanged a tender gaze, silently conveying the emotions that words couldn't express. The bus ride felt both eternal and fleeting, filled with anticipation and a sense of longing.

When my stop finally arrived, I gathered my courage and spoke, "I had a wonderful time today, Arjun."

He smiled as he responded, "Even I had a great time. Take care and reach home safely."

With a heart filled with joy, I bid him goodbye and stepped off the bus, cherishing the memories of this unforgettable day and looking forward to the next chapter of our love story.

36

Courage Amid Chaos: A Battle for Freedom and Happiness

01 February 2014

On January 16, 2014, a cold winter day, I left my in-laws' house just a few days before my second marriage anniversary. The past year's struggles weighed heavily on my mind, leaving me apprehensive about the future. My family had become aware of the turmoil I had endured and was determined to help me find a way out of this suffocating situation.

As January unfolded, I lived in constant fear, fearing that I might be forced to return to that oppressive environment. However, my family, ever persistent in resolving the matter, attempted to converse with Ajay, my estranged husband. They hoped to find a peaceful settlement, a way for both parties to move forward. But to my astonishment, Ajay's response was far from what I had expected.

"Heartache can be forgotten, but only if Kumudh holds my leg and apologises," he declared, his words laced with bitterness. His demand struck my family like a thunderbolt, shattering any remnants of hope they had held onto. It became evident that reconciliation was an impossible dream, and the path to freedom lay elsewhere.

With a heavy heart, we decided to initiate divorce proceedings. I knew this choice would throw my life into a whirlwind of chaos, but deep down, I believed it was the only way to reclaim my happiness. Material possessions meant little to me, for what I truly valued was the unwavering support of my family.

Gathering strength from their love, I took a leap of faith, determined to reshape my destiny. The journey ahead would undoubtedly be arduous, but it was a journey towards self-discovery and liberation.

In our pursuit of emancipation, we demanded our rightful jewellery and full custody of Aarav, our precious son. It was not just a battle for our freedom but a fight to ensure a secure and loving environment for our little one. The courtroom became the arena where our hopes and dreams clashed with the bitter realities of life.

Amidst the legal proceedings, my physical health took a toll. Once invisible and forgotten, the stitches from my c-section now throbbed with pain, demanding my attention and care. Bedridden for a month, I was forced to confront the consequences of my choices. But even in my weakest moments, my family stood by me, offering solace and taking care of Aarav, who, too, had experienced the discomfort of a tender stomach.

As I lay in bed, healing physically and emotionally, I marvelled at the resilience and strength that had brought me this far. The road ahead was uncertain, but the flickering flame of hope burned brighter within me than ever before. I knew that no matter how challenging the path, I would rise from the ashes of my shattered marriage, embracing the freedom and happiness that awaited me.

Little did I know that this rest period would catalyse the transformation unfolding. The whispers of change grew louder with each passing day, and the time had come for me to rise, reclaim my life, and rewrite my destiny.

ᐳᐳᐳ

(After two months)

After filing for divorce, my life changed, but one thing remained constant—I continued to wear my Mangalsutra. Despite the dissolution of my marriage, I held onto this symbol of tradition and womanhood. It profoundly spoke to me, reminding me of my cherished cultural heritage.

"Mangalsutra, After all the fucking incidents ?" I (Ankit) asked, my voice tinged with surprise.

Kumudh nodded, a small smile playing on her lips. "Yes, I did. It's not about holding onto the past but embracing the traditions and values that resonate with me."

I furrowed my brow, clearly puzzled. "But isn't that contradictory? You filed for divorce, yet you wear a symbol of marriage?"

Kumudh took a moment to gather her thoughts, searching for the right words. "Marriage is not just a legal bond; it encompasses many emotions and experiences. Wearing my Mangalsutra reflects my appreciation for the sacred institution of marriage and its role in my life, even if it didn't last forever. It's a reminder of the love and commitment I once had and the lessons I've learned along the way."

My eyes widened with surprise as I glanced at Kumudh 's neck, noticing the absence of her mangal sutra. I couldn't help but ask, my voice tinged with curiosity, "Kumudh, I noticed you used to wear your Mangalsutra. Did you stop wearing it after you split?"

Kumudh paused momentarily, her gaze fixated on a distant memory, before responding, "No, Ankit. This was one incident when Aarav played around and accidentally uprooted my Mangalsutra. It was completely unexpected, and I lost it in the following chaos."

ᑭᑭᑭ

(After 1 year)

Life has a way of testing us, pushing us to our limits and revealing our true strength. Over the past year, I've come to understand my resilience and embarked on a journey of self-discovery. During the most challenging times, we truly get to live an authentic life.

I found solace in my work at a school where I could positively impact young minds. The smiles on their faces and the joy in their laughter filled my heart with contentment. I found happiness and fulfilment in this newfound role, forging a unique mine path.

Living as a single mother was difficult, but I proudly wore that title. I embraced the challenges and responsibilities that came with it, knowing I could provide my child with a loving and nurturing environment. Each day, I juggled my roles as a mother and an individual, finding a delicate balance between the two.

Now, my life has two intertwined aspects. First and foremost, I have become my own priority. I prioritise my well-being, my dreams, and my growth. I indulge in self-care, pursue my passions, and carve out moments of happiness. Second, I believe that everything happens for a reason. Life's twists and turns have taught me valuable lessons, guiding me to understand myself and the world around me better.

In this new chapter, I stand tall as a single mother, confident and determined to make the most of every opportunity.

37

Defying Judgment, Embracing Freedom: A Divorcee's Journey

"What about your life after your divorce?" I asked, genuinely curious. Although the topic of divorce always seemed daunting, I was eager to hear her perspective.

"Free, independent, happier?" she replied with a sense of liberation. Hell yeah, free, independent, and happier," she emphasised to reassure herself.

"It must have been a challenging decision to make," I commented, trying to better understand her experience.

She nodded thoughtfully. "Life works out when your choices and decisions are right for you. Accepting the pain, trauma, and sorrow of divorce is essential," she explained, her voice tinged with wisdom and resilience. "Nobody enters a marriage with any idea about breaking it. Everybody hopes it is for life. And yet, sometimes, this happens."

I couldn't help but ponder her words. It was true; life had its unexpected twists and turns. "In some ways, life can be more problematic," I ventured cautiously, considering the potential challenges she might have faced.

Her response was swift and confident. "But it depends on you. What voices you heed depends on you," she asserted, her tone firm. "What about the social repercussions?" I asked, aware of the societal judgments that often accompany divorce.

A knowing smile crossed her face. "There are, of course, also social repercussions. Most people fear this the most. The tag of being a divorcee is fearful and often considered worthy of contempt. And yet, in my experience, people are very varied," she explained, her eyes shining with resilience. "I have found people who condemn me and my family, and who support me. What I know from experience is that life is full of potential. We meet new people, and our perceptions change all the time."

Her words resonated deeply. They reminded me that people's opinions should not define one's path. "Some people judge, and they always will," I said, empathising with the unsolicited advice that often comes with such situations.

She nodded in agreement. "There is unsolicited advice. My response, through my actions (more often than words) and words, has been, 'It is my life, my choices, and none of your business,'" she stated confidently, a hint of defiance in her voice. "Divorce made me look at relationships anew. The decision taught me resilience."

As I listened, I couldn't help but admire her strength. "It sounds like it taught you a lot about yourself," I observed, realising the transformative power divorce could hold.

Her gaze turned introspective. "It taught me a lot about myself. Now that I have tasted life without those bounds, I can never return," she confessed, a mix of gratitude and determination evident in her voice.

At that moment, I understood that her divorce had not only been an ending but also a beginning—a catalyst for self-discovery and personal growth. Her journey reminded me that life could take unexpected turns, but our response to those challenges genuinely shapes our happiness and independence.

*****

As a divorcee, it's been more than two years now since the end of your marriage. During this time, you've experienced various challenges that many women in similar situations can relate to. I will ask you a series of questions, and let's catch your responses:

Pity:

"People have shown fake sympathy and compassion towards me, but I haven't fallen for it. They say things like, 'You must be lonely, right? How do you stay active? I hope you're able to find someone suitable.' However, I haven't discussed the details of my divorce with anyone because I know they won't truly understand unless they've been through it themselves."

Judgment:

"I've faced judgment for everything, from what I wear and eat to who I talk to. It used to bother me, but I've learned to keep calm and ignore it. Besides, I must wear a Saree in school as it's compulsory, sometimes inviting even more judgment."

Facing the fact:

"Now that I'm a divorcee, the world never misses an opportunity to remind me of that status. It's a constant presence in my life."

Curiosity:

"My sex life remains a source of mystery to others, and I prefer to keep it that way. I've never discussed it with anyone because they won't believe what I say and will create their version of the truth."

Adjustment:

"I've changed my personal and professional life since the divorce. I prioritise eating healthily, caring for myself, and keeping busy."

Learning to be alone?

"This aspect has been challenging. However, my family has been a tremendous support in helping me overcome the difficulties of being alone."

Self-pity:

"I've realised the need to stop indulging in self-pity. If I don't stay strong, I'll be crushed. I've come to understand that I am all I have and must rely on myself."

Ankit: Faith?

"Just because I've gone through tough times doesn't mean I've lost faith in myself or a higher power. I still believe in my abilities and the strength to overcome obstacles."

Family and Aarav?

"My family is my lifeline. They have been there for me throughout this journey. As for Aarav, he holds a special place in my heart."

Dating?

"Yes, I have started dating again.

Ahh, Arjune, I added.

Although my family knows it, I haven't openly discussed it with them, Kumudh added with a slight smile on her cheeks.

38
Raindrops of Intimacy: Unveiling Mandav's Secrets

"So you didn't reply to him when Arjun proposed to you that night?" I (Ankit) asked, my eyes filled with curiosity.

Kumudh sighed, contemplating how to express her feelings. "Yes, I didn't answer him that night," I admitted, my voice tinged with a hint of hesitation.

I leaned closer, my brows furrowing in confusion. "But why? Are you interested in him or not?" I probed, seeking answers to the questions burning in my mind.

"Wait, let me finish, Ankit," Kumudh replied, a touch of determination creeping into her voice. "I didn't respond to him that night, but something changed between us after that night. We decided to go on a one-day trip to Mandav."

My eyes widened, and my curiosity piqued even further. "Mandav? That's quite a leap from a simple proposal," I remarked, a mix of surprise and intrigue colouring my words.

Kumudh nodded, a soft smile gracing her lips as she recalled the memories. "Indeed, it was unexpected. We embarked on this journey to unravel the unspoken emotions lingering between us. It was a chance to truly get to know each other without the distractions of everyday life."

I leaned back, absorbing my words, envisioning our adventure. "So, what happened during this trip? Did it change anything between you two?" I inquired, eager for every detail.

As Kumudh reminisced about that eventful day, a glimmer of excitement danced in her eyes.

ᐅᐅᐅ

---Mandav---

June – 2017

We arrived in Mandav on a picturesque Monday, surrounded by the lush greenery that concealed several couples lost in their little worlds. It had been a long time since I set foot in this place, perhaps around eight years ago in 2009, accompanied by the fuck, man...

I found myself playing the role of a guide, narrating the captivating history of each fort to my companion, Arjun. We captured the beauty of our surroundings through countless photographs, freezing those precious moments in time.

Eventually, we decided to take a break and find a cosy spot to sit down. Arjun began speaking as we settled, but my attention wavered when I saw a signboard transporting me back to 2009. Realising that I was sitting in the same place I had visited all those years ago was a surreal experience.

Lost in nostalgia, the sky above darkened, and rain clouds formed. A light shower interrupted our reverie, adding a touch of romance to our day. Embracing the unexpected rain, we allowed ourselves to get drenched before seeking shelter in a secluded spot to dry off.

As the rain seeped through my light-shimmering Kurti, I noticed Arjun stealing glances at my bosom. Although I didn't mind his gaze, I made no effort to conceal myself, inadvertently giving him the impression that I desired more. In a bold move, he caught my arm, pulled me towards him, and planted a passionate kiss on my lips, forging a deep connection between our souls.

It was the first time I had experienced such an enchanting kiss with a man. Encouraged by the moment, Arjun attempted to explore further by slipping his hand beneath my Kurti, but I hesitated when his touch reached my navel.

"Arjun, not now," I softly pleaded, wanting our lovemaking to be an incredible experience that would unfold naturally, a mutual exploration of pleasure and intimacy. I envisioned secret rendezvous in the middle of the night, where we would surrender to our desires, revelling in the knowledge that our love was both dangerous and exhilarating.

Respecting my wishes, Arjun withdrew his hand and proceeded to shower me with gentle kisses, grazing my neck, head, and eyes. Meanwhile, my hand ventured across his perfectly chiselled chest, appreciating his exquisite physique. Despite our clothes remaining on, the tingling sensations and sparks between us grew more robust, as if our bodies were intimately entwined.

Arjun's readiness for more became evident, but a distant laugh shattered our trance just as we got lost in the moment's intensity. Suddenly, self-consciousness crept in, causing us to pull away and instinctively lose that fleeting instant of connection.

Taking a deep breath, I gathered the courage to speak my heart. "Arjun, I love you too," I confessed, running my fingers through my hair as if attempting to smooth out the uncertainty and anticipation in the air.

Remember,

You are the shining star in your parent's eyes,

Never break down for anyone.